LOOKING AT OLD PRINTS

W R Southwarpe fecit   London Pub by J Kendrick 54 Leicester Sqre
                                         Sept. 1833.

JOHN versus JACK.

Looking at Old Prints

John Booth

1983

CAMBRIDGE HOUSE BOOKS
WESTBURY, WILTSHIRE

FIRST EDITION

© John Booth 1983

ISBN 0 906853 036

769.942

Photoset and Printed
in Great Britain by
Redwood Burn Limited
Trowbridge, Wiltshire
Bound by
Macdermott & Chant Ltd
Enfield, Middlesex

Happiness is in the taste, not in the thing;
And we are made happy by possessing what we
ourselves love,
Not what others think lovely.

Rochefoucault

Acknowledgements

Many friends, collectors and dealers have contributed to the experience that has made this book possible and to them I send sincere thanks. During my early days as a print collector I had the good fortune to meet W. L. Richardson, who was for many years on the staff of a major London print gallery. His lifelong knowledge of old prints, and kindly response to my ignorance of the subject, turned him into a great personal friend and an ideal mentor. At about this same time I was lucky enough to meet Bath bookdealer and printseller John Stanton, who contributed my first lesson on print cleaning and subsequently supplied some of my first books on collecting. Through John I also met another Bath specialist, John Gough, whose skill as a researcher of old prints and watercolours first brought home to me the importance of this aspect of collecting.

In more recent times my interest in the plate making techniques used by the early print makers has been greatly assisted by the practical knowledge and skill of the professional engraver W. P. Sinclair, whose wildlife studies have earned him an enviable international reputation as a decorative steel engraver. I am also indebted to Professor Michael Twyman for his comments on William Millington and his work with an early Senefelder printing press; and to Mr. F. L. Wilder who assisted my research and kindly gave permission for me to quote from his informative book *How to Identify Old Prints*—one of many reference sources that have contributed to my knowledge and enjoyment of the subject.

I now don my publisher's hat in order to pay tribute to the people who have assisted with the making of the book. The sheer competence, courtesy and kindness of John Rivers and his staff at Redwood Burn during all the various stages of the book's production has virtually matched the pleasure I derived from writing it! Finally, thanks are due to Marie Naish for typing the manuscript; to my brother Tom, for so speedily correcting the draft and making many useful suggestions, and Marion Barton for her two-day marathon in preparing the index. I am especially grateful to my family, for their encouragement and support, and to my wife Pam for putting up with the chaos and disruption to the household furnishings whilst the book was being written.

Contents

	Page
List of Illustrations	11
Foreword by the Marquess of Bath	15
Author's Note	17
Origins of Print Making in Britain	21
Print Making Processes	45
Print Collecting	73
Prints and Print Makers including:	
Cornelius Caukercken	96
William Hogarth	98
James Seymour	100
George Edwards—John Gould	102
Smith of Chichester	104
Paul Sandby RA	106
Thomas Gainsborough RA	108
Samuel & Nathaniel Buck	110
Jean Baptiste Le-Prince	112
Thomas Ryder	114
James Gillray	116
Joseph Stadler	118
John Raphael Smith	120
Thomas Rowlandson	122
George Morland	124
Samuel Drummond ARA	126
William Henry Pyne	128
William Daniell RA	130
Thomas Girtin	132
Joseph Mallord William Turner RA	134
William and George Cooke	136
Lowes Dickinson	138
Samuel Prout	140
Henry Alken	142
Thomas Miles Richardson	144
Thomas Sutherland	146
James Pollard	148

James Duffield Harding 150
Eugene Delacroix 152
David Lucas 154
Thomas Sidney Cooper RA, CVO 156
Thomas Shotter Boys 158
John Harris 160
Charles Eden Wagstaff 162
William Millington 164
Edward William Cooke RA, FRS 166
Thomas Goldsworth Dutton 168
H. Guest 170
William Simpson 172
Myles Birket Foster RWS 174
Thomas Picken 176
Mrs. Jane Wells Loudon 178
Carlo Pelligrini 180
'Graphic' Cricketers—1890 182
Terms Used in Print Collecting 185
Bibliography 187
UK Dealers in Old Prints 191
Index 197

List of Illustrations

Frontis.   'John v. Jack' by W. R. Sculthorpe—etching.

No. 1   Print from the *Nuremberg Chronicle*—hand coloured woodcut.

No. 2   Map of Glamorgan by Christopher Saxton—line engraving.

No. 3   Portrait of William Camden by Robert White—line engraving.

No. 4   Map of Kent from Michael Drayton's *Polyolbion*—line engraving.

No. 5   Title page from Blaeu Atlas—line engraving.

No. 6   Copper-plate printing press—courtesy of Thomas Ross & Son & Michael Twyman.

No. 7   Lord Arundel by Wenzel Hollar—etching.

No. 8   Dutch Men O' War by Wenzel Hollar—etching.

No. 9   The Earl of Danby by Valentine Green—mezzotint.

No. 10   Saint Francis by William W. Ryland—stipple engraving.

No. 11   View of Stonehenge by J. Jeakes—aquatint.

No. 12   Scraps from the sketchbook of Henry Alken—soft ground etching.

No. 13   The Midland Railway—St. Pancras—wood engraving.

No. 14   Lithograph by Alois Senefelder.

No. 15   William Millington's lithographic press (*courtesy Houlton Bros., Trowbridge*)

No. 16   Sir Robert Peel by George Baxter—Baxter print.

No. 17   Line engraving techniques—ancient & modern.

No. 18   Cawood Castle Gateway by J. Rogers—line-etching.

No. 19   Uncle Toby & the Widow by Lumb Stocks RA—line engraving.

No. 20   Simon, Lord Lovat by William Hogarth—etching.

No. 21   Lord Clive by Francesco Bartolozzi RA—stipple engraving.

No. 22   Plate from *Liber Veritatus* by Richard Earlom—mezzotint.

No. 23 A Summerland by David Lucus—mezzotint.

No. 24 Hunting the Stag by H. Harrel—wood engraving.

No. 25 South East View of Longleat after W. Wheatley—lithograph.

No. 26 Print from Baxter type oval key-plate—aquatint.

No. 27 Enlargements of print making techniques a) line engraving; b) stipple; c) mezzotint; d) aquatint

No. 28 King Charles II by Cornelius Caukercken—line engraving.

No. 29 Marriage-à-la-Mode after William Hogarth—line engraving.

No. 30 A Hunter taking a Flying Leap after James Seymour—copper line engraving.

No. 31 Birds by George Edwards and John Gould a) etching; b) lithograph.

No. 32 Original etching by Smith of Chichester.

No. 33 Worcester by Paul Sandby RA—aquatint.

No. 34 The Gipsies by Thomas Gainsborough RA—line-engraving & etching.

No. 35 South Prospect of Berwick on Tweed by S & N. Buck—etching.

No. 36 Vue des Environs de Nerva by J. B Le Prince—aquatint.

No. 37 Visit to a Woman of the Lime Trees by Thomas Ryder—stipple engraving.

No. 38 'The Feast of Reason & the Flow of Soul' by James Gillray—etching.

No. 39 London from Lambeth by J. C. Stadler—aquatint.

No. 40 His Royal Highness George Prince of Wales by J. R. Smith—mezzotint.

No. 41 'The Glutton' by Thomas Rowlandson—etching.

No. 42 The Country Butcher after George Morland—photo-mechanical reproduction.

No. 43 Mr James Asperne after Samuel Drummond ARA—stipple engraving.

No. 44 Study of Waggons by W. H. Pyne—etching & aquatint.

No. 45 A View of Amlwch Harbour by William Daniell RA—aquatint.

No. 46 View of the Village of *Chaillot* by Thomas Girtin—soft ground etching & aquatint.

No. 47 Basle by J. M. W. Turner RA—mezzotint.

No. 48   Lechlade by G. Cooke—line etching.

No. 49   John Booth by Lowes Dickinson—lithograph.

No. 50   Fountain of the Stone Cross, Rouen after Samuel Prout—
           aquatint.

No. 51   'Turning the Man Boney Couldn't Turn' after Henry
           Alken—aquatint.

No. 52   Grey Street, Newcastle by T. M. Richardson—lithograph.

No. 53   Lord Howe's Victory June 1st, 1794 by Thomas
           Sutherland—aquatint.

No. 54   The Mailcoach in a Storm of Snow after James Pollard—
           aquatint.

No. 55   High Street, Edinburgh by J. D. Harding—lithograph.

No. 56   Un Forgoron by Eugene Delecroix—aquatint.

No. 57   The Lock by David Lucas—mezzotint.

No. 58   Animal Study by T. S. Cooper RA—lithograph.

No. 59   The Tower of London by Thomas Shotter Boys—
           lithograph.

No. 60   Royal Artillery by J. Harris—aquatint.

No. 61   The Marriage of Her Majesty Queen Victoria by C. E.
           Wagstaff—line engraving & stipple.

No. 62   Market Place, Trowbridge by William Millington—
           lithograph.

No. 63   The Thames, East Indiaman by E. W. Cooke—etching.

No. 64   The 'Lincolnshire' by T. G. Dutton—lithograph.

No. 65   Mardon's Shooting Gallery by H. Guest—aquatint.

No. 66   Charge of the Light Cavalry Brigade after William
           Simpson—lithograph.

No. 67   The Toy Boat, Miles B. Foster RWS—chromo-lithograph.

No. 68   Bath Ford by Thomas Picken—lithograph.

No. 69   Wild Flowers by Mrs Louden—lithograph.

No. 70   The Marquis of Bath by Carlo Pellegrini—chromo-
           lithograph.

No. 71   Some Representative Cricketers—'Graphic' 1890—wood
           engraving.

Foreword

by

The Marquess of Bath

'Ah! what pleasant visions haunt me'

Longfellow

Stored away in our country houses, libraries and museums, often far from the public gaze, lies a part of our artistic heritage much forgotten and unexplored. The world of prints and print-makers we have ignored too long and thereby lost much treasure. It is a great pleasure, therefore, to present to you the chance to delve more deeply into this hidden art.

John Booth's fascinating book spans the 400 years dividing Tudor England from the reign of Queen Victoria. Dealing first with the origins of print-making in Britain, he moves on to print-collecting as a hobby—where to obtain prints, how to look after them, how to detect forgeries—illustrating all with a delightful selection of examples of the work of some of England's best print-makers. With its lucid explanations and lively style, and above all, its superb illustrations, here is a book to capture the imagination of any newcomer to this field.

Don't miss the 'Vanity Fair' cartoon of my illustrious grandfather!

Bath

Author's note

My introduction to print-collecting was the result of happy accident when buying our present home some twenty years ago. We discovered the previous owners had left behind a quantity of books and pictures and a surprising offer from a local antiquarian bookseller caused us to review our 'finds' with something more than a passing interest.

Since that initial awakening, the collection has grown considerably and some of the prints are now amongst our most treasured possessions. Each has its own story to tell, apart from providing a fascinating pictorial record of personalities, places and events of a Britain long since forgotten.

You don't have to be an expert to become a print-collector but the newcomer will find that as the interest quickens so the knowledge grows. There is infinite scope for the young and the not so young, whether one pays a few pounds for one of the delightful steel-engravings of the last century, or a small fortune for some Regency masterpiece.

If yours is just a passing interest, I hope you enjoy looking at old prints as much as I enjoy collecting them.

June, 1983   J.A.B.

The Origins of
Print Making
in Britain

The Origins of Print Making in Britain

A study of old prints ought to begin with some understanding of the various hand worked plate making techniques that were used to produce them and this should enable the various processes to be identified. A variety of materials were used to make the plates and blocks, including wood, metal and stone on which the design was carved, scraped, etched, engraved or drawn. An inked impression printed on paper, or other suitable material, employing any of these methods or materials is termed an **original print**. This definition cannot, of course, apply to modern photographic reproductions, regardless of whether they carry the signature of the artist or not. If an item can be authenticated as having been printed at least one hundred years ago, it is customary to refer to it as an **antique print**.

The terms used to describe the various printing techniques will, at first, seem strange to the layman, but they are relatively few in number, namely: woodcuts, wood engravings, line engravings, drypoints, etchings (including stipples, soft-ground etchings and aquatints), mezzotints and lithographs. The notes used in the chapter on Print Making Processess are based on those prepared for local education authority courses and regular seminars on old prints held at various venues. If they are used with the related illustrations, the reader should have no difficulty in identifying the various processes that were used.

The following brief outline may assist the reader to appreciate the historical development of print making in Britain and the contribution old prints have made to the social and cultural life of our nation.

The earliest examples of printed illustration are the **woodcuts** that illustrate the books of William Caxton and his successor, Wynkyn de-Worde, and date from the late fifteenth century. The prints they contain were made from hand-carved wood blocks and are, for the most part, crude, inartistic, and of little interest to today's print collector. Complete volumes in good condition command high prices due to their historic importance and interest.

One of the important early books of this period was the *Liber Cronicorum* (1493), better known as the Nuremberg Chronicle. This mighty tome was the fifteenth century's attempt at an illustrated history of the world and contained over 1,800 woodcut illustrations for which a mere 654 blocks were employed.

21

No. 1   Print from the *Nuremberg Chronicle*—hand coloured woodcut
Author's Collection

The woodcut used to depict Paris (Plate 1) was the same as that used for both Dante and Thales and came from a hand coloured copy of the book that cost three times the price of the original edition when it was published in 1495. This suggests that the hand colouring of prints is a practice as old as printing itself, possibly the natural successor to the hand illuminated works that played such an important part in the convent and monastic life of the kingdom.

The first printed atlas of the world was published at Bologna in Italy in 1477, based on the researches of Claudius Ptolemy (100–178 AD). There can be few authors whose work survived for more than one thousand years before publication. The copper plates from which these maps were printed were prepared by a process known as **line engraving**, a method of incising designs on metal by means of a burin or graver, a sharp pointed engraving tool. The art of engraving on metal for ornamental purposes had long been practised by goldsmiths before its use as a printing process was discovered. Line engraving was already well established in Europe prior to its introduction here in the mid-sixteenth century. In Britain its early use was confined mainly to title pages and portrait frontispieces as, for example, the fine portrait of Queen Elizabeth that adorns Christopher Saxton's famous *Atlas of England and Wales*, published in 1579. This book was the great publishing achievement of 16th century Britain and was the first national Atlas of its kind to be produced in any country.

The maps were printed from copper line engravings (Plate 2) and despite the many foreign engravers who by this time were working in Britain, several were produced by native engravers, namely Francis Scatter, Nicholas Reynolds and Augustine Ryther. Ryther was to become one of the first of a new generation of print sellers, his 'Shoppe being a little from Leadenhall next to the sign of the Tower'. Sadly, this business venture failed and 1595 was to see him installed in the Fleet prison for debt.

Two other engravers who belong to this important early British

No. 2   Map of Glamorgan by Christopher Saxton—line engraving
Author's Collection

No. 3   Portrait of William Camden by Robert White—line engraving
Author's Collection

School were William Rogers and William Hole. Little is known of Rogers, but his portrait of Queen Elizabeth (Eliza Triamphans) engraved in 1689 to mark, it is thought, the defeat of the Spanish Armada, is possibly the first portrait engraved by an Englishman. He also prepared the title page for an edition of Camden's *Britannia* published in 1600.

William Camden, the great Elizabethan historian, is worth more than a passing mention. The new edition of his *Britannia*, published in 1607, included a set of line engraved maps of the English and Welsh counties. The title page and twenty-one of the fifty-seven maps together with a number of pages of early British and Roman coins were engraved by William Hole. In my copy of his history there is a rather splendid portrait of Camden in his state uniform as Clarenceux King of Arms, engraved by Robert White (1645–1704) (Plate 3). As the work is dated 1637, it rather looks as if Robert White was a mere eight years of age when he engraved it! Subsequent research has revealed that the portrait originally appeared in a 1695 edition from which it had been removed to grace the earlier book. William Hole engraved music (the first Englishman to do so) and the title pages and portraits for a number of other books of the period. He produced a rather curious set of pictorial maps adorned with nudes, nymphs, shepherds and the like, which appeared in Michael Drayton's *Polyolbion*, first published in 1612, (Plate 4) and now a rare collector's book.

By the 17th century it was established practice to issue books with engraved title pages and portraits (Plate 5). This process required a different kind of printing press from the one used to print text (letterpress) and led to the increasing use of the copper plate press. Instead of installing these presses, many general and book printers sent their copper plate work to firms equipped with these machines and a degree of specialisation arose which is still with us today. As the demand for illustration increased, it became accepted practice to print in excess of the quantity ordered and a lively business developed in maps and portraits. This resulted in the establishment of two new trades—the publisher and the print seller. Both were to add impetus to the demand for copper plate work, although the presses used in this period were very basic in design and somewhat primitive in operation. Most were fitted with a central screw, operated by a kind of windlass which, when rotated, lowered the top clamp on to the bed of the machine. Printing plate and paper were thus brought together under very considerable pressure. Too little pressure and a weakly-inked impression resulted; too much, and the copper plate might crack or break, with the loss of

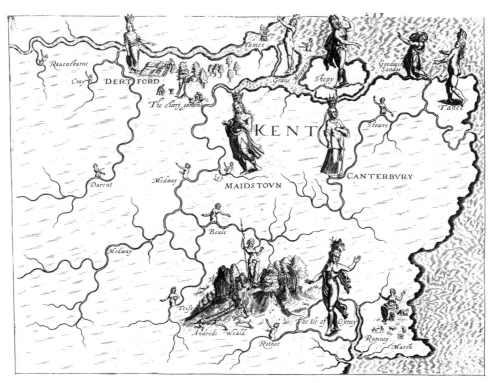

No. 4   Map of Kent from Michael Drayton's *Polyolbion*—line engraving
Author's Collection

months of valuable engraving time.

Despite the remarkable advances made in printing technology since the 19th century (the text for this book was set by computer), the design and operation of the copper plate press has altered little. Work on today's machines is still very much a manual operation, involving the hand-inking of the plate before each impression is taken. The press rather resembles an overweight, oldfashioned clothes mangle (Plate 6). Nevertheles, its contribution in the field of printed illustration has been remarkable, enabling the work of past generations of artists, etchers, and engravers to be preserved for posterity.

The rise of **etching** in Britain owes much, if not all, to the influence of one man—Wenzel Hollar (1607–77). Hollar, a native of Prague, arrived here in 1636 as a member of the household of Thomas Howard, Earl of Arundel, one of His Majesty's (King Charles I) principal Ministers of State (Plate 7). The Earl was a great patron of the arts and realised that in Hollar he had found an etcher of outstanding ability. Sadly, less than ten years later, both the Earl and Hollar had to flee the country when the

26

No. 5   Title page from Blaeu Atlas—line engraving *Author's Collection*

Royalist cause foundered. Fortunately, by this time Hollar had already etched a great many plates, including portraits of the Royal Family and many of the nobility and gentry of the period. It was during his enforced exile in Holland that he etched the delightful series of Dutch Men O' War and other sailing vessels (Plate 8).

In etching, a copper plate is first covered with a wax ground and a fine needle set into a wooden handle is used to draw the design on the plate, penetrating the wax to the copper beneath. The artist/etcher has much greater freedom of movement whilst preparing the design than does the line engraver who must physically cut each line into the plate. The etcher's work can be completed in hours, compared to the weeks, months or even years required to complete a large or very detailed engraving.

The completed plate is now ready to be 'bitten' and the edges and back are sealed with a special varnish resistant to acid attack, and the plate immersed in a bath containing dilute nitric (or similar) acid. This attacks the areas exposed by the etching needle and bites the line work into the plate, producing an effect similar to that achieved with a graver. When the plate has been bitten to the required depth it is removed from the bath, washed in clean water and printing can commence.

There is little or no apparent visual difference between an incised line

No. 6 Copper plate printing press (*courtesy Thomas Ross & Son/Michael Twyman*)

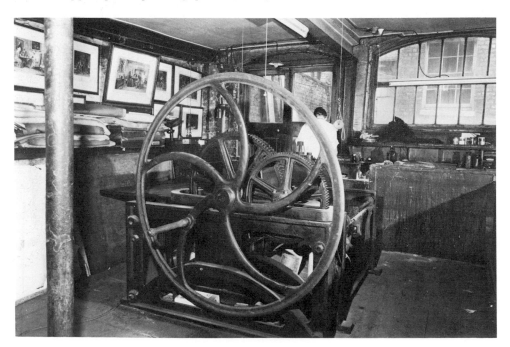

ILLVSTRIS: & EXCELLENT. D: DOMINVS THOMAS HOWARD, COMES ARVNDELIÆ & SVRRIÆ
primus Comes & summus Marescallus Angliæ &c nobilissimi ordinis Garterij Eques, Serenissimi po
tentissimiq Principis Caroli, Magnæ Britanniæ Franciæ & Hiberniæ Regis, Fidei defensoris, &c. in Anglia, Sco
tia, et Hibernia a Secretioribus Consilijs et ejusdem Regis A 1639. Contra Scotos Supremus & Generalis Militiæ P

Ant: van Dyck Eques pinxit.   W Hollar fecit 1646

No. 7   Lord Arundel by Wenzel Hollar—etching *Author's Collection*

29

No. 8   Dutch Men O' War by Wenzel Hollar—etching *Author's Collection*

that has been etched and one that has been line engraved. There are, however, certain characteristic differences between the two techniques and the appearance of a particular print can usually provide the keen observer with sufficient evidence to enable him to decide whether it has been etched or line engraved (see Print Making Processes).

Despite the influence of Hollar, it seems there was very little interest in etching in Britain after the Restoration. Some important work was undertaken by a small handful of native etchers of whom Francis Barlow (c. 1626–1703) is the most famous. Barlow is credited with the earliest print of a horse race, published in 1687, and dedicated to 'King Charles II . . . of blessed memory'. Barlow was probably the first British etcher whose work was used for book illustration. His earliest known example in this field is Benlowe's *Theophila* in 1652. This was followed by the plates for an edition of *Aesop's Fables* in 1666, many of which are thought to have been destroyed in the Great Fire of London. Several of the delightful vignettes that adorn the road maps of John Ogilby's *Britannia* of 1675 have a Barlow 'feel' about them. Hollar engraved the frontispiece of this famous work based on a drawing by Barlow. Both men undertook work for Richard Blome, the important 17th century publisher. Hollar's inferior work on Blome's maps is in sharp contrast to the great ability he displayed on the Ogilby frontispiece. Blome's major contribution to 17th century Britain was the publication of the

30

Gentleman's Recreation in 1686, with views of hawking, hunting, shooting and other field sports compiled from drawings made by Barlow. Blome thus became the first publisher in a now long-established tradition of British sporting books, although this particular work is now rare and costly.

Francis Place (1647–1728) was an amateur etcher of note who worked after Barlow's animal and bird studies. A native of York and a man of private means, he is said to have refused the King's commission and a fee of £500 per annum to make drawings of the vessels in the Royal Navy. In common with Barlow, the examples of his etched work are now difficult to find.

The important print making process known as **mezzotint** was introduced into Britain by Prince Rupert (1619–82) on his return from exile after the Restoration. The art was first practiced by Ludwig von Siegen who, like the Prince, was a soldier and an officer in the service of the Landgrave of Hesse. The Prince was fascinated by the new technique and working under the guidance of von Siegen produced several plates by the new method. Subsequent development in Britain was at first confined to portraiture, the first dated mezzotint being that of King Charles II engraved by William Sherwin and published in 1669.

Mezzotint was later to become the engraving process at which we in Britain excelled. If our native line-engravers in the eighteenth century appeared crude and primitive in comparison to their continental neighbours, this was possibly because many of them were involved in the production of the fine mezzotint portraits of the period. The technique enabled the works of portraiture and landscape to be reproduced with a tonal quality not possible by any other process until the introduction of aquatint in the late eighteenth century. Mezzotint collecting became the vogue (Plate 9) and work by some of the leading exponents of the art changed hands at astronomical prices. At one sale in 1901 a mezzotint portrait of the Duchess of Rutland, by Valentine Green, realised over £1,000, whereas the original by Sir Joshua Reynolds was painted for a fee of 150 guineas!

The early mezzotints were worked on copper plates with all the inherent limitations that this material placed on the size of the editions. The first step in the process was to 'ground' the plate and for this operation the engraver used a tool called a 'rocker'. With it he traversed the plate, working at first horizontally across the surface, then vertically and, finally, diagonally. The sharp file-like teeth of the rocker ploughed into the surface of the plate producing a rough finish, not unlike the feel of coarse sandpaper.

HENRY DANVERS EARL OF DANBY

No. 9   The Earl of Danby by Valentine Green—mezzotint *Author's Collection*

32

Work with the rocker was far from popular and tended to be boring and time consuming, the task usually falling to a senior apprentice or journeyman. From this basic operation originated the well known phrase 'off his rocker'—possibly an indication of the stress sometimes caused by this tedious early work on the plate. An inked impression, taken after this grounding process was completed, would print black and there was a velvet-like feel to the ink that can still be detected today, if one has the good fortune to find an early example in fine condition.

The plate then passed to the mezzotint engraver who commenced to scrape up the highlights, working from dark to light with a sharp scalpel-like tool. This scraping process demanded great sensitivity and skill; the more a particular area was scraped, the smoother it became, thus reducing its capacity to retain ink at the printing stage. The light areas on a portrait, including the flesh tints, were treated in this manner and so would print white, due to an absence of ink. This ability to depict light and shade by scraping resulted in the tonal excellence and almost photographic quality of many of the fine portrait mezzotints of the 18th and 19th century.

Early practitioners included Francis Place, the etcher previously mentioned, Isaac Becket, George White, John Smith and William Faithorne, the younger. The art was to continue its active development until the early 1720's when it went into decline. Its fortunes were revived around the middle of the century by the establishment of a new school of mezzotint engravers, working in London and lead by a young Irishman, James McArdell (c. 1728–65). His skill and enthusiasm carried the craft to new levels of perfection and assured its continued use as the principal reproductive medium for portraiture and, to some extent, landscape, for the next one hundred and fifty years.

Many fine mezzotint portraits and some landscapes (often printed in colours) were still being produced during the early years of the twentieth century. These are only now beginning to find favour with collectors, despite their excellent quality and undoubted rating as original works of art.

In common with most of the old print processes, mezzotint engraving went into decline with the invention of the camera and the introduction of photogravure in the latter half of the nineteenth century. Prints from these relatively modern mechanical processes will doubtless be looked upon as antiques by future generations. They, in all probability, will find it difficult to accept that the complicated hand worked plate making skills described here were possible, let alone practised.

The technique of etching mentioned earlier was to play an important part in the development of a new engraving technique known as **stipple engraving** (or engraving by dots), believed to have been introduced by the famous engraver William Wynne Ryland (1732–83). Certainly, Ryland can lay claim to the introduction of engraving in the chalk or crayon manner, of which stipple engraving was a subsequent development. He prepared many of his early prints by using a narrow roulette wheel for much of the detail, and may have worked with this through a wax ground on the plate, a much speedier process than directly engraving the plate.

Many of Ryland's prints were printed in red or brown ink and the example (Plate 10) is dated 1764, published when he was 32 years of age. He was later executed at Tyburn for forgery, on 29th August, 1783.

The stipple process is really an adjunct of etching and the plate was provided with a wax ground in the same manner as etching. The dotted detail was pricked through the wax with an etching needle and bitten by immersion in acid. It was the practice to re-enter or deepen the dots with engraving tools, including the punch and graver.

The rise of stipple engraving in Britain owed its popularity to the school of Bartolozzi (1725–1815) and the many engravers who worked with him were to produce nearly two thousand plates over a period of about thirty years. Several important mezzotint engravers were attracted to the new technique, including Richard Earlom (1743–1822), John Raphael Smith (1752–1812), and the brothers, William (1766–1826) and James Ward (1769–1859).

The attraction of stipple prints for today's collector is probably due to the fact that many were printed in colours and display a definitive quality generally lacking in hand coloured examples. In order to achieve this, coloured inks were applied directly by hand to the printing plate which was cleaned off and re-inked after each impression. For this reason, no two examples of the same print are exactly the same. This colouring of the plate added considerably to the cost. The attractive appearance of many of the larger stipple prints enable them to command high prices when they come on the market. It is possible that their original popularity was due to their attractiveness when printed in colours, rather than to any real appreciation of stipple engraving as a process on the part of the print buying public.

Two men who made important contributions to the development of print making during the latter period of the eighteenth century were Paul Sandby (1725–1809) and Thomas Bewick (1753–1828). Sandby's ability as a painter in watercolour was matched by his ability as an etcher. He is also credited with the introduction of the **aquatint** into

34

No. 10   Saint Francis by William W. Ryland—stipple engraving
Author's Collection

Britain, a process first practised by the French painter-etcher Jean Baptiste Le Prince (1733–81).

Examples of Sandby's early topographical works are reproduced in publications of the late 18th century, including Kearsley's *Virtuosi's Museum* and Walker's *Copper Plate Magazine*, which he shared with other notable artists of the early English watercolour movement, including John Varley, J. M. W. Turner and Thomas Girtin. Sadly, none of the copper plates in these publications were produced by the aquatint process, but they are tending to gain in value as their importance to the art historian is recognised. Aquatint, like mezzotint, is a tonal engraving process and pure examples of either are never supported by the use of outline etching. It is probably the most complicated print making process to master and resulted in the establishment of a specalist class of aquatint engravers, of which the Daniell and Havell families are the best known.

The process is complicated for the layman to understand but it enjoys the merit of being one of the easiest to identify, although prints produced by this technique are costly and difficult to find. Many of the fine

No. 11   View of Stonehenge by J. Jeakes—aquatint *Author's Collection*

sporting, maritime and topographical prints of the last century were produced by the aquatint process and can be recognised by their cellular-like texture evident on the dark or shaded areas of a print (Plate 11).

With aquatint, acid is used to 'bite' in the tonal values on a plate as opposed to etched lines. The light areas, including the sky, are varnished over and the plate is returned to the acid bath for further biting. As the various areas on the plate are bitten to the desired depth, consistent with the tonal quality required, they are stopped out with varnish, the dark areas being left until last. As many as twenty immersions were required on some plates, the complicated 'stopping out' procedure being necessary after each meeting with the acid.

Unlike the mezzotint, where the engraver works from dark to light, the aquatint engraver works from light to dark. The ink values are, of course, the same; lightly bitten areas, such as skies, retain minimal ink, tending to print white; heavily bitten areas are deeper and retain more ink and so print black. The appearance of the cellular-like quality of aquatint (I call them 'bobbles'!) is described under Print Making Processes.

Some authorities claim that aquatint reached its zenith in the 1830's and then began to decline in favour of lithography, a new process introduced into Britain in the early 1800's. A great many aquatint copper and steel printing plates are still in existence. Prints from these are sold quite legitimately by the printers concerned as modern 'pulls' from original plates. An increasing number are however finding their way into the salerooms, suitably 'aged' in the hope of catching the unwary. This is reason enough for the inexperienced collector to seek the advice of a reputable professional dealer until such time as he is able to rely on his own knowledge and judgement.

Soft-ground etching was popularised by Henry Alken (1784–1851), a famous sporting artist of the early 19th century. The technique had previously been practised to good effect by Thomas Gainsborough (1727–88), although examples of his work are rare and expensive. Some of George Morland's (1763–1804) work was also reproduced in soft-ground and may still be bought quite cheaply. Henry Alken used the process to good effect on many of his smaller sporting prints and for book illustrations (Plate 12). These display a soft, pencil-like quality very similar in appearance to lithographs, with which they are often confused. Sadly, prints from Alken's sketch books are sometimes hand coloured by dealers, thus destroying something of their value as original works of art.

Soft-ground etching is similar to etching except that a special ground,

Scraps from the Sketch-book of Henry Alken. Engraved by himself.

No. 12   Scraps from the sketchbook of Henry Alken—soft ground etching
Author's Collection

with a high tallow content, was used on the plate. The artist made his design on a piece of drawing paper which was then placed over the plate and retraced with a pencil. The paper was pulled gently away from the plate and particles of wax from the ground adhered to the back of the paper, corresponding to the traced outline. The plate was then bitten by acid in the usual way.

Two other important printing processes were developed in the early nineteenth century, **wood engraving**, re-introduced by Thomas Bewick (1753–1828) and lithography, a method of reproducing drawings made on stone tablets, invented by a German, Alois Senefelder (1771–1834) in 1798.

Bewick, a native of Newcastle, was trained as a line engraver but adapted his skill to engraving on wood. His books, illustrated by wood engravings, are classics; *A General History of Quadrupeds*, published in 1790 and his *History of British Birds*, published in two volumes in 1797 and 1804.

In wood engraving the design is first drawn on the end grain of a suitably prepared block of wood and the surrounding material is cut away, leaving the design to be printed standing out in relief, not unlike the lettering on a rubber stamp.

The great merit of this method of illustration is that the blocks can be incorporated with the letterpress (text) and both printed together on the same machine (Plate 13). The traditional copper plate press with its slow and laborious method of operation could not meet this new challenge. Despite the introduction of steel printing plates, which enabled individual illustrations to be printed in thousands, rather than the hundreds of the copper plate era, these manually operated machines could not compete in a world that was becoming increasingly mechanical. By the mid-19th century the delightful topographical plate books of previous decades, with their charming steel engravings of bustling city streets and rural landscapes, had all but disappeared.

The discovery of **lithography** by Alois Senefelder (1771–1834) in the late 18th century (Plate 14) was to revolutionise the printing industry

No. 13   The Midland Railway—St. Pancras—wood engraving
Author's Collection

and provide the basis for a process that is today responsible for something like ninety per cent of the output of the British printing industry. Lithography is a planographic system, that is to say the drawing to be printed lays on the surface of the stone, little pressure (a kiss) being required to print from it. For this reason plate-marks will not be found on original lithographs. A great many artists were attracted to the new technique which enabled them to make original drawings and then reproduce them in unlimited quantities.

The process relies on the principle that oil and water do not mix. The artist worked on a specially surfaced piece of limestone, drawing his design with a greasy pencil. On completion of the drawing the top of the

No. 14   Lithograph by Alois Senefelder *Author's Collection*

Henry Monnier.   lith: de Senefelder.

Aou Diable les amis qu'on ne connait pas!

May the Devil fly away with intimate friend's whom we do not know.

No. 15　William Millington's lithographic press
(*courtesy Houlton Bros., Trowbridge*)

stone was treated with a solution of diluted acid which was repelled by the greasy drawing but attacked the surrounding stone. The stone was then soaked with water and printing ink applied by roller. The ink from the roller would not adhere to wet limestone but was attracted to the grease of the drawing. Provided the stone was kept moist and the design regularly inked, almost unlimited copies could be made.

A Wiltshire man, William Millington of Trowbridge, was one of the first provincial printers to use one of Senefelder's lithographic presses (Plate 15) and was already working with the process in the early 1830's. He was a competent artist and produced a number of topographical lithographs of Wiltshire views that are now scarce and valuable. An example of his work is included in the collection.

Thomas Shotter Boys (1803–74) issued a magnificent series of prints of London. James Duffield Harding (1798–1863) also produced many fine lithographs, mostly of a topographical nature. The important animal painter, Thomas Sidney Cooper (1803–1902), also worked in the medium. The work of all these artists is now very popular with today's print collector.

No. 16   Sir Robert Peel by George Baxter—Baxter print *Author's Collection*

This new process provided a serious challenge to aquatint and many fine prints on every conceivable subject were produced. A number depict the industrial and commercial ventures of the age, including the building of railways, bridges, and the important passenger-carrying steam vessels of the Brunel era. These, together with the topographical lithographs of the period, provide a valuable and important historical record of 19th century Britain prior to the development of photography.

A major printing breakthrough of the 19th century was the introduction of mechanical colour **printing in oil colours** introduced by George Baxter (1804–67) in 1835. This process combined both methods of intaglio and relief printing; a mezzotint or aquatint master plate (usually the latter) and a series of wood blocks used to print the various colours (Plate 16).

Baxter patented his process and for some years jealously restricted its use to his own firm. For something like twenty-five years he printed an unlimited variety of high quality colour prints depicting all aspects of life in Victorian Britain. When he ceased business in 1860, much of his plant and stock-in-trade was bought under the hammer by other printers including Le Blond, one of his licencees. Original Baxter prints are now scarce and valuable. Needless to say, many clever forgeries exist which are fairly easy to detect (see Print Making Processes).

Subsequent experiments in photography by Fox Talbot at Lacock in Wiltshire, and by Daguere in France, led to the eventual introduction of printing plates that utilised the photo-mechanical processes of gravure and lithographic printing and paved the way for the colour and high quality printing techniques of the present day.

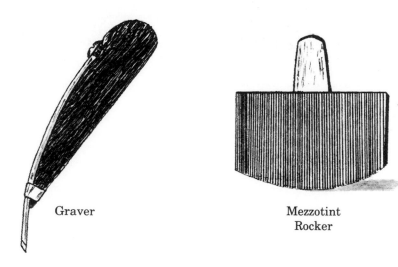

Graver

Mezzotint
Rocker

Print Making
Processes

Print Making Processes

Line engraving

Line engraving was the first *itaglio* print making process to be practiced in Britain (pronounced in-tal-i-ow), an Italian word which means to incise. All prints where the image to be printed is below the surface of the plate are known as intaglio prints and include all variations of etching and also mezzotints. In Britain during the 16th century printing plates were made from copper sheet, the work on a single plate taking many months and sometimes years to complete!

The engraver worked with a lozenge-shaped pointed graver or burin with the plate resting on a sandbag, enabling the plate to be rotated in either direction as he worked. The illustrations (plate 17) are photographs of a present day engraver working on a plate (fig. 1) and also attempting to work with the graver in the manner described by Abraham Bosse in his book on engraving techniques published in 1645 (fig. 2). Most reference works since Bosse's original treatise (including many modern ones) claim that the graver was held and manipulated in the manner Bosse described, i.e. with the forefinger resting along the top of the blade, the graver being pushed forward and downward away from the engraver.

Today's engravers regard this technique as unsatisfactory because complete control over the graver is difficult, if not impossible, when held in this way. The printing industry has a traditional reputation for jealously guarding the secrets of its craft skills. Did Bosse really break with this tradition in his book, or was this a deliberate attempt to mislead the curious, perhaps to the delight and amusement of his fellow engravers?

All prints produced from intaglio plates display plate-marks. This is an impressed outline on the paper surrounding the print and is caused by the great pressure of the printing press on plate and paper during the printing operation.

In the 16th and 17th centuries the hand beating and preparation of the thin copper sheet used for plate making was very expensive and engravers ordered plates only fractionally larger than the outer border of the item to be engraved. These tolerances increased from about $\frac{1}{8}''$ (3mm) in the 1580's to something like $\frac{3}{8}''$ (9mm) a century later. By the closing years of the 18th century, they had become even more generous (as methods of producing copper plate improved) with plate-marks often

46

(Fig 1.)

No. 17 Line engraving techniques—ancient & modern

(Fig 2.)

as much as $\frac{3}{4}''$ (19mm) away from the engraved border. A study of these plate-mark variations is quite fascinating and can sometimes greatly assist the serious collector in determining the age and authenticity of an item.

The use of copper had, however, one inherent disadvantage; the rapid surface wear to the plate brought about by repeated printings. This resulted in a loss of definitive quality in the lightly engraved areas on the plate (because these were nearer to the printing surface) after a few hundred impressions had been printed. This limitation is the reason why copper-plate engravings tend to be much scarcer and more expensive than their later steel counterparts and also why the fine engravings and illustrated books of the copper-plate era are now so expensive. It was general practice to rework or re-engrave worn plates and sometimes this remedial work was not carried out with anything like the skill displayed on the originals. Many 17th century map plates were re-worked in this way and this probably accounts for some of the elderly features on the cherubs that adorn some later issues of Blaeu and Jansson maps.

Soft steel began to replace copper for plate making in the early eighteen-twenties and, although this was much more difficult to engrave, the plates were far more durable. One of the first engravers to make use of the new material was the famous mezzotint engraver Samuel Cousins (1801–87), reputed to have engraved his first plate on steel in 1820. The following forty years may be said to have represented the golden age of line engraving in Britain, despite the challenge brought about by the expansion in wood engraving. Steel plates were much cheaper to produce than the copper previously used and plate-marks became increasingly generous, often several inches away from the print itself. Where prints were intended for use as book illustrations their large paper margins were sometimes trimmed to conform to the size of the book and the plate-mark was lost. Steel was, of course, a very hard wearing material and enabled several thousand impressions to be printed from a single plate without any serious loss in definitive quality.

Line engraving on both copper and steel was used as a volume method of producing copies of drawings and paintings. There are quite different characteristics between prints made from copper and those made from steel. In the case of copper, the detail tends to be somewhat heavy and laboured with a total absence of fine line work (Plate 18). Steel, as the harder material, lent itself to much finer engraved detail and this is very noticeable on topographical prints where the fine engraving of skies is unlikely to be appreciated without the aid of a magnifying glass. A

48

No. 18   Cawood Castle Gateway by J. Rogers line-etching *Author's Collection*

characteristic of line engraving is the extent to which the engraved detail completely covers the entire surface of the plate.

A typical example of steel line engraving is that of 'Uncle Toby and the Widow' (Plate 19), a delightful mid-Victorian steel engraving by Lumb Stocks R.A. (1812–92), one of three plates he engraved on this same

No. 19   Uncle Toby & the Widow by Lumb Stocks R.A.—line engraving
Author's Collection

subject. The engraver's skill in contrasting areas of light and shade is clearly evident on this print; the methods used to achieve this may not be quite so obvious. The dark areas often betray heavier line work (a graver with a wider point) or the use of cross hatching. This criss-cross pattern by increasing the number of lines, increased the density of the ink in certain areas and a darker printed image resulted. The lighter area on the left knee has been burnished (rubbed out) and this loss of engraved surface is unable to retain ink and is highlighted by printing white. There is similar skilled treatment to the other leg. Here the shadow cast by the coat is cleverly introduced by the use of cross hatching.

Although 19th century line engraving is regarded as interpretive and therefore lacking in originality, there is no escaping the technical ability of the engravers who produced it. Despite their skills, they were barred from membership of the Royal Academy. The engraver of this particular print, Lumb Stocks R.A. (1812–92), may appear to have been an exception to this rule but he was admitted to membership in his own right as a painter. It is uncommon to find a print where both artist and engraver were Royal Academicians. In the case of Stocks, his outstanding ability as an engraver dwarfed his skill as a painter and he is likely to be remembered more for his work with the graver than with the paint brush.

Notes on line engraving

Line engraving was the first intaglio print process to be practiced in Britain.

Itaglio means to incise, i.e. printing image below the surface of plate.

In line engraving the entire surface of the plate is covered with line-work.

All intaglio plates have plate-marks, minimal in the 16th century; as much as $\frac{3}{4}''$ away from engraved surface by late 18th century.

Early printing plates were made from copper sheet. The soft nature of the material restricted print runs to a few hundred copies. Soft-steel introduced for plate making after 1820.

The re-working of copper plates was common practice.

Several thousand impressions were taken from steel plates without serious loss of engraved surface.

Usually possible to determine from a print whether it has been produced from copper or steel plate.

Steel plates have much wider plate-marks than copper but these were frequently trimmed off.

19th century line engravers usually copied the work of important
artists.

Line engraving considered a craft skill—i.e. engravers were not usually
admitted to membership of The Royal Academy.

Etching was (and still is) a method of producing illustrative printing
plates by allowing acid to bite through a design prepared on the wax-
ground of a metal plate. An etching needle was used to draw the
illustration, the needle penetrating the wax to the metal beneath. The
edges and underside of the plate were sealed with varnish to prevent
them being attacked by the acid and the plate was immersed in a bath of
dilute nitric or similar acid. The acid ate into the metal of the plate that
had been exposed by the etching needle, producing an incised image on
the plate. This technique substituted the time consuming role of the
graver (used in line engraving) for the speedier corrosive action of acid
upon metal.

After the plate had been bitten to the satisfaction of the etcher, it was
removed from the acid bath and washed in hot water to remove any
remaining wax and all traces of acid. An ink charged dabber was
employed to work the ink into the incised areas of the plate which was
then wiped to remove all traces of surface ink. Printers often used the
palm of the hand to 'ball the plate' in order to ensure that no traces of ink
remained on the surface. It is now thought that this action was
responsible for a good deal of the subsequent plate wear that resulted
when printing from copper plates.

Since the days of Hollar, etching has been practiced by a great many
important artists, the medium providing a freedom of movement with
the etching needle almost as unrestricted as pencil work. Many etchings
are not unlike pen-and-ink drawings in appearance and a popular
misconception still exists with many that this is what they are. As
intaglio prints they possess plate-marks and in general terms comply
with the remarks made earlier about the use of copper and steel for plate
making.

It is important that the reader should appreciate the difference
between *original etching*, where the artist-etcher himself prepared and
executed the design on the plate, and *interpretive etching*—a copy by an
etcher of the work of someone else. Quite obviously, an original etching
made by a well known artist has an intrinsic art value far greater than a
copy.

The reader may care to compare the *etched* portrait of Lord Lovat,
etched by William Hogarth in 1746 (Plate 20), with a similar *line-*

No. 20   Simon, Lord Lovat by William Hogarth—etching *Author's Collection*

engraved portrait, that of Uncle Toby on page 50. The Lovat portrait almost meets the criteria of a line engraving (ie. a plate completely filled with engraving) except for the open detail on the face and clothing. It is a good example of the freedom and sketch-like possibilities presented by this particular art form, although it must be admitted that much of the line work and cross hatching betray Hogarth's earlier training as a line engraver.

Lord Lovat was purchased at a local rummage sale in 1965 for the princely sum of half-a-crown. Time and experience has established that the etching comes from a reasonably early printing, many Hogarth plates being re-worked and re-issued on a number of occasions. It is pleasing to possess an original etching by an artist of the importance of William Hogarth, who made the etching only hours before Lord Lovat was beheaded for Treason. There are a number of rather interesting etchings in the collection that are perhaps more typical of the etchers' style than is this example. Sir Seymour Haden, the famous landscape etcher is reputed to have once said 'in etching never use two lines where one will do'.

A great many of the small topographical prints that appeared in the illustrated books of the late 18th and early 19th century were etched in the style of line engraving and often the wording 'Engraved by...' appears beneath them. Perhaps some publishers during that period were under the impression that they were paying for the more costly process of line engraving! These prints are so different from the original etchings that will be reviewed later, that it is possibly more satisfactory (and certainly less confusing) to regard them as line engravings (Plate 18). There is a certain compatibility between the two techniques and it is not uncommon to find many examples where both are combined on the same print.

Drypoints and soft-ground etchings

Drypoint etching is a method of producing intaglio prints where the etching needle serves as a graver, the plate being incised in a manner similar to line engraving. As the copper is 'ploughed' by the needle, a 'burr' is raised either side of the line. Unlike line engraving, this burr is allowed to remain on the plate and produces a delicate feathery effect when the etching is printed. However, the metal soon breaks down with the printing operation and the likelihood today of finding drypoints taken off early pulls from a plate are somewhat unlikely. These items

54

are, however, rather a specialised area of print collecting and somewhat beyond the scope of this book.

Soft-ground etching, as previously explained in the introduction, is also an intaglio process but here a special ground containing an excess of tallow was used. The drawing was made on paper with a soft pencil which was placed over the wax ground of the plate and re-drawn. When the paper was carefully pulled away from the plate particles of the wax ground adhered to the back of the paper. The technique resulted in a soft pencil-like effect when the etching was printed which, incidentally, was bitten in exactly the same manner as a normal etching. The soft-ground etching previously illustrated (Plate 12) from the sketch book of Henry Alken is the only example of this technique included in the collection.

Soft-ground etchings that have had their plate-marks cut off can quite easily be mistaken for lithographs. In such cases research is difficult unless the print carries a signature or publisher's imprint which can be traced to a suitable reference work. Books on the subject are, of course, vital to the serious collector. The writer has something over two hundred on print collecting but there are still serious gaps.

Stipple prints and aquatints

Both processes have close ties with etching and good examples of either are increasingly difficult to find. It is customary to describe stipple as engraving by dots but much background detail, particularly on stipple portraits, carries a great deal of both etched and line-engraved work.

The stipple portrait of Lord Clive (Plate 21) by Bartolozzi is vastly superior in appearance and technique to that of Hogarth's Lord Lovat made some forty years earlier. The work on the Lovat plate was possibly a labour of hours, compared with the many months of detailed and complicated effort on the larger stipple plate. Many stipple prints display dark granular backgrounds, not unlike aquatint in appearance, and they are sometimes confused with mezzotints by the layman. They are unlikely to be aquatints for few portrait aquatints were ever produced in Britain. With a suitable magnifying glass a mezzotint print will reveal the minute and delicate cross hatching on the flesh tints of the subject, caused by the action of the rocker. These are quite different from the dots or granular appearance of stipple prints or aquatints.

Aquatint was possibly the most complicated and time consuming of the various print making techniques to be introduced. Its popularity, coupled with the difficulty of the process, led to the establishment of a school of engravers who specialised in the art. Although it is customary to refer to 'aquatint engraving' no engraving was involved, the process relying on the use of acid to bite a printing plate to varying depths. The original idea behind the introduction of the process was an attempt to

No. 21   Lord Clive by Francesco Bartolozzi R.A.—stipple engraving
Author's Collection

produce prints in the style of watercolours, although the 'aqua' possibly relates to aquafortis (nitric acid), for the prints are acid-tints.

The process employed small particles of resin that were dusted onto a prepared copper plate to which they attached themselves when the plate was heated. This was immersed in acid and the resin particles, being impervious to acid attack, remained attached to the plate, the acid biting into the surrounding areas. An alternative method of preparing an aquatint ground was to dissolve resin in alcohol which, on evaporation, left the resin deposits on the plate. The resin contracted on drying, producing a miniature crazy paving effect throughout the surface of the plate. These numerous islands of resin (cellular, not dots) can be clearly observed particularly in the shaded areas of aquatints.

In biting the plate the light areas were treated first (for example, skies) and then the plate was removed from the acid bath, washed off and the sky stopped out with the acid resistant varnish. A great many immersions in the acid bath were required with various parts of the plate being stopped out each time the plate was removed. The aquatinter worked from light to dark, the final biting being the darkest areas of the composition. The tonal quality of the work was developed so that at the printing stage the lightly bitten areas carried minimal ink, printing almost white, while the deeply bitten areas carried larger ink deposits and printed black.

Notes on etching

All forms of etching are intaglio prints and display plate-marks.
The process relied on use of acid to bite design into plates.
Practiced in Britain from 17th century.
Original etching—artist prepared and executed the design.
Interpretive etching—etcher copied the work of another.
Some etchings were produced in the manner of line engravings—i.e. etched detail completely covering the surface of the printing plate.
William Hogarth undertook original etching.
Original artist's etchings often display minimal linework.
A mixture of etching and line engraving is common to many prints.
Drypoint etching uses needle as a graver, raising burr. Only limited print runs were possible due to loss of surface burr.
Soft-ground etching not unlike soft pencil work—and similar to lithographs in appearance.
Stipple prints display dotted pattern, particularly on flesh tints.
Aquatint introduced by J. B. Le Prince (c. 1769).

Aquatints—method of etching employing resin particles and repeated bitings. Tonal process, but frequent use made of etched line work. Displays cellular composition, particularly in shaded areas.

Mezzotint

The various print making techinques were mentioned at some length in the opening chapter to enable the layman to appreciate where each fitted into the general pattern of print making in Britain. A fairly detailed explanation of the *mezzotint* process was given and the reader will recall how the copper plate was prepared by the use of a surrated rocker, followed by a lengthy period of hand scraping to produce the various tonal values on the plate.

From the time the process was introduced into this country by Prince Rupert it was extensively used for portraiture, a medium to which it was ideally suited. It is probably true to say that the British engravers did for mezzotint what the French did for copper line engraving and British mezzotint engravers became the envy of their European neighbours. Many fine sporting prints were produced in the medium by J. R. Smith, the Wards and others working after George Morland's paintings. The prints were frequently printed in colours by a direct application of the various coloured inks to the printing plates. These prints have considerable decorative merit and appeal and continue to command high prices in the salerooms. Not surprisingly a great many forgeries were produced in the early years of the present century by photo-mechanical means, after which the prints were cleverly coloured by hand. If the layman has opportunity to see a genuine mezzotint printed in colours its brilliant appearance will prevent any future mistakes.

An example of a photo-mechanical copy of *The Country Butcher* by Morland is included in the collection and reviewed later in the book.

The first important British engraver to use the mezzotint process for the interpretation of landscape was Richard Earlom (1723–1822), whose plates after Claude Lorraine's *The Liber Veritatis* were published by John Boydell in 1777 (Plate 22). Earlom's extensive use of outline etching is clearly visible on this example, which has the appearance more of an etching than a mezzotint and perhaps underlines the unsuitability of this technique for the rendering of landscape.

This combination of outline etching with mezzotint appears to have found favour with J. M. W. Turner R.A. (1775–1851), who from about 1821 began to issue the plates of his *Liber Studiorum* in exactly the same

58

No. 22   Plate from *Liber Veritatus* by Richard Earlom—mezzotint
Author's Collection

manner as Earlom, even to printing the edition in the same reddish
brown inks used by the former engraver.

It may, perhaps, be helpful at this point to say a little about the tonal
processes of mezzotint and aquatint and what is meant by references to
pure mezzotint or *pure aquatint*. Both processes rely on the ability of the
engraver to produce a design on a plate displaying a total absence *of line
work* of any kind. To outline etch a tonal engraving is to destroy
something of its merit and rather defeats the object of the process.

On the mezzotint example of *A Summerland* by David Lucas (Plate
23), the entire engraving is devoid of line work. Similarly, the aquatint
of Stonehenge (Plate 11) and also that of *Un Forgeron* by Delecroix have
both been executed with a total absence of outline etching. The reader
can judge for himself whether these pure examples of process are able to
stand on their own merit as skillful renderings of tonal engraving
without the need for etched outlines.

Despite the advances made in modern printing techniques, prints of
this kind present all kinds of problems for today's book printer. Firstly,
many of the illustrations have to be drastically reduced in size from that

No. 23　A Summerland by David Lucas—mezzotint *Author's Collection*

of the originals. Secondly, the 'fuzzy' nature of both mezzotint and aquatint defy the camera's ability to reproduce them clearly in order to provide the printing plates. This can be partly overcome by the use of a screen which breaks the picture into a series of dots, thus improving its definitive quality, but at the same time introducing a pattern on the illustration not present on the original.

The execution of important landscape subjects in *pure* mezzotint had to await the work of David Lucas (1802–81) with his powerful renderings of John Constable's (1776–1837) paintings. Two large Lucas mezzotint prints are in the collection, including *The Lock* which is illustrated. It may be that Constable tried to repeat the success that Turner enjoyed with the publication of prints after his drawings and paintings. Unfortunately, Constable's prints met with even less enthusiasm than did his painting, and his publishing venture, which he personally financed, lost him a great deal of money.

Mezzotint continued in vogue throughout the nineteenth century and where the engravers confined their work to portraits of the famous there was a ready demand. Samuel Cousins R.A. (1801–87), William Say (1768–1834) and Thomas Lupton (1791–1873) have each, in turn, been credited with the introduction of steel plates. Cousins was certainly the most skilled worker in mezzotint and whilst he executed a great many plates on steel, the new material somehow lacked the lustre and delight of earlier work on copper.

Notes on mezzotint

Introduction of mezzotint by Ludwig von Siegen (c. 1642).
Process introduced into Britain by Prince Rupert after the Restoration.
Tonal process employing rocker-work and scraping.
Mainly used for portraiture in the 17/18th centuries and some landscape in the 19th century.
Some plates printed in colours but many hand-coloured fakes issued in early 20th century.
Important landscape works include:
    Earlom   *The Liber Veritatus*
    Turner   *Liber Studiorum*
    Lucas/Constable   *Various subjects of Landscape.*
Lucas mezzotinted all works after Constable.
Landscape mezzotint was frequently supported by etched line work.
Pure mezzotint carries no etched line work.
First mezzotint on steel plate produced in 1820.
Samuel Cousins R.A., most skilled mezzotinter of the 19th century.

Wood-cuts and wood engraving

There is a considerable difference both in style and cutting technique between the somewhat primitive wood-cuts of earlier centuries and the wood engraving of the Bewick period. As a **relief** print making process, the undoubted merit of wood engraving was that illustration and text could both be printed on the same machine—the letterpress. The blocks were no longer carved from the plank, as in former times, but were produced from either boxwood or a variety of fruit-woods, the engraver working on the end grain of the material. The tools were similar in appearance to the gravers used for line engraving but the intaglio printing principle was reversed with incised lines printing white and raised areas printing black.

The identification of wood engravings presents some problems for the new collector, typical examples being not unlike line engravings or etchings in appearance. The reader may find the following comments will assist with identification. Wood engravings being made by a **relief**

No. 24   Hunting the Stag by H. Harrel—wood engraving *Author's Collection*

printing process are without plate-marks. Credits to artist and engraver do not normally appear below the print as is usual on line-engravings. The signature of the wood-engraver often appears on the print itself, usually printed in block capitals in the right-hand bottom corner, like that of H. Harral on the one illustrated (Plate 24). If the reader is in doubt about the identity of a particular print a little cheating is permitted that has nothing to do with the appearance of the print. The title beneath the item is almost certain to have a letterpress caption. This was invariably set from the standard type forms available to the printer and looks 'modern' in comparison with the engraved titles on other prints.

The increased use of wood engraving in the Victorian era owed its popularity to the magazines and periodicals of the period of which *Punch* and *The London Illustrated News* are possibly the best known. Unlike many book illustrations, the periodicals of the day were printed with letterpress text on the back of the prints and this frequently shows through, affecting the quality of the illustration.

Due to the increasing scarcity of original line engravings, some print-dealers are now colouring and framing wood engravings of the last century. Many of these portray important social or historical events and are usually priced quite cheaply, whereas similar examples made by lithography or aquatint are likely to be expensive. Very often these wood engravings can provide useful information for the postal historian or for the collector in a field other than print collecting where a particular illustration may relate to the collector's interest.

The demand for wood engraved illustration in the 19th century became so great that firms began to specialise in the supply of bulk orders to publishers. The Dalzeil brothers and Swains are two firms who produced volume work of high quality and whose names are found on many of the blocks issued during that period. Work on a large block or, perhaps, one illustrating a recent battle or disaster where urgency of publication was essential would demand a composite approach. Here the block would be made in several parts, each being given to a different engraver. When the engraving was completed, the sections were bolted together ready for printing in a quarter of the time normally taken to engrave the whole. The trained eye of the experienced collector can usually detect the joint lines on some of these composite examples. The writer has an original block depicting the Vinegar Works at Worcester circa 1840, complete with smoking chimneys and works railway. The urgency that lead to such a block being produced in this manner is a matter of speculation.

Wood-cuts and wood engravings were produced by relief printing—there are no plate-marks.

Wood-cuts were the first illustrative prints to be produced and date from the discovery of printing.

Early examples are somewhat crude and uninteresting and apart from certain notable examples are of little interest to today's print collector.

Wood engraving owed its popularity to the original work of Thomas Bewick in the late 18th century and became a major illustrative medium in the 19th century particularly for magazines and periodicals.

The technique enabled both illustration and text to be printed on the same machine.

The prints are not unlike line engravings and etchings in appearance but carry letterpress captions.

Wood engravings from periodicals usually carry text verso which often shows through the paper and spoils the illustration.

Due to the scarcity of original engravings some dealers are now hand-colouring and selling wood engravings.

Composite engraving allowed several engravers to work on the same block in order to reduce production time. Joint lines can often be detected on prints produced in this manner.

Lithography, or printing on stone (lithos-Greek for stone), was discovered at the close of the 18th century by a German, Alois Senefelder, (pronounced Zane-velder) in 1798.

This **surface**, or **planographic**, method of printing relied on the principle that oil and water do not mix. In simple terms the early form of the art consisted of producing a drawing with a greasy crayon on the specially prepared surface of a limestone block. The porous surface of the stone was soaked with water which was repelled by the greasy drawing. Similarly, when an inked roller was passed over the surface, the ink was attracted by the drawing but repelled by the moisture present in the surrounding undrawn areas of the stone. Providing the stone was kept moist and a regular ink supply was maintained, an almost unlimited supply of prints was possible.

The process suffered one major disadvantage, the handling and storage of the large blocks of limestone on which the illustrations were prepared. The stone needed to reproduce the print of Longleat (Plate 25) would be three times the size of the drawing and at least 6 inches

No. 25   South East View of Longleat after W. Wheatley—lithograph
Author's Collection

(150mm) in thickness. The efforts of at least two workers would have been necessary to move it to the press. On really large stones a chain hoist and trolley were used and the job of locating the stone on the press was a major lifting operation.

Unlike prints produced by the intaglio process, where often the metal printing plates would survive for centuries, the litho drawing would be erased from the stone after printing and a new drawing would be substituted. The possibility of re-printing an item was thus eliminated unless a drawing on the stone was retained. This explains the rarity of many lithographs today, particularly those produced by small provincial printers as was this example. Although printed in London for the firm of W. C. and J. Penny of Frome, it is unlikely that this order called for more than a few hundred copies.

Uncoloured lithographs are similar in appearance to soft pencil drawings and the natural grain of the stone was frequently used in the composition and looks something like pencil shading. Early examples often carry the wording 'Drawn on stone by . . .' together with the name of the lithographic firm printing the item. Early practitioners included Charles Hullmandel, who introduced litho-tint, Louis Haghe and the firm of Day & Son.

65

A number of important artists working in the 19th century used lithography for reproducing their work, including J. D. Harding, James Ward, T. G. Dutton, T. S. Cooper, Samuel Prout, J. A. Gould, T. S. Boys and J. C. Bourne. Many of these original artists' lithographs are now rare and expensive.

Hullmandel introduced the basis of colour printing to lithography (chromo-lithography) by the use of a second or tint-stone that provided the print with a biscuit-coloured background wash. Pinholes on the corners of early lithographs betray the registration points that were used to locate the print on the tint-stone. The process reached its zenith in the late 19th century by which time as many as twenty different tint-stones might be used on the production of a single print.

Modern printing processes are almost all based on this original printing concept but the transmission of colour is now achieved by a photographic process which shows up as a series of fine regimented dots (see frontispiece). Old coloured lithographs printed from stones betray no such dotted pattern and are not unlike original watercolours for which they are frequently mistaken!

If an old black and white lithograph is reproduced by modern lithography a nearly exact copy of the original is possible as the screening (dot) process is unnecessary. Usually the paper used will alert the experienced collector. Some clever hand coloured copies are finding their way into salerooms suitably aged and abetted by battered frames— cuncullus non facit monachum.

Notes on lithography

A surface or planographic printing technique developed by Alois Senefelder in 1798 which allows a greasy drawing made on limestone to be reproduced in almost unlimited quantities.

Relies on principle that oil and water do no mix.

Process used by a number of important British artists in 19th century.

Editions were frequently 'limited' due to drawings being erased and stones used for other graphics as soon as a job was printed.

Original lithographs produced by many provincial printers were usually printed in small editions and are now rare.

Tinted lithographs introduced by Hullmandel in early 19th century were the fore-runners of colour printed lithographs. A separate stone used for each colour. Register pin-holes are visible on corners of early examples when tint-stones were employed.

Examples printed in colour may sometimes be mistaken for watercolours.

Modern examples printed in colour display tiny dots which carry the colour.

A dotted pattern, whether monochrome (black & white) or coloured (chromo-lithograph), indicates a modern process.

Modern copies printed in *monochrome* can be printed without a dot pattern and when hand-coloured may look very like originals.

Baxter prints

For a period of something like twenty five years in the mid-Victorian period a somewhat indifferent British public had the opportunity to own and enjoy some of the finest examples of colour printing ever produced, resulting from the efforts of George Baxter (1804–67). Baxter was little recognised in his own country, except by imitators, but widely acclaimed abroad.

His unique method of print making combined an intaglio keyplate (printed on a copper-plate press) with a series of wood engraved blocks that transmitted the brilliant oil colours to the prints via hand operated letterpress machines. Unlike present day methods, the keyplate was printed first and the various coloured blocks were superimposed over it with a breath-taking accuracy of registration that was Baxter's hallmark.

An interesting and unusual collecting find made by the writer some years ago was an uncoloured print taken from an oval keyplate. A closer inspection of the print (Plate 26) revealed that it was from a worn aquatint plate which appeared to have been re-worked on a number of occasions. The employment of aquatint would certainly account for the excellent definitive quality of many of Baxter prints.

Due to the wear on the plate this example has been reproduced as a half-tone to improve the quality of the illustration. Had this been produced in colour the dotted structure of the print would have been even more apparent. Despite this, a great many Baxter prints were forged in the early 20th century by exactly this method of reproduction. The reader should employ a good magnifying glass on any suspect examples bearing in mind the maxim 'if it's dotted, it's a dud'. The fact that the print may be set in what appears to be a genuine embossed Baxter mount is merely an attempt to aid the deception.

Several of Baxter's contemporaries tried in a variety of ways to produce work in colour by methods similar to those used by him. The writer has a copy of *The Art Journal*, published in January 1851, containing an example of colour printing from wood blocks by George Leighton, originally one of Baxter's apprentices. The print is titled,'*The Hawking Party*' (after Landseer) and provides an interesting but somewhat less attractive contrast to the work of his old master. Happily, some print dealers appear blissfully unaware of the importance of this particular print, an example complete with mount having been recently purchased for a five pound note.

Another 19th century colour printer who attempted work in a style very similar to Baxter was Charles Knight. Two volumes of his *Old England*, bought many years ago for pence rather than pounds, contain a number of interesting coloured wood block illustrations. His key-plate was, however, printed on the same letterpress machine but was applied after the colour had been printed. This interesting work is only found in the first edition published in 1845 and is readily identified by the illuminated title page.

Baxter produced numerous portrait prints of the Royal Family and of the famous and important people of his day (Plate 16). This example of Sir Robert Peel, founder of the Police (hence the term 'bobby' or 'peeler') is untrimmed on one side. The register holes used to locate the print over the wood blocks are clearly visible. A new point was necessary for each block used, otherwise the holes would become enlarged and so destroy the accuracy of register which was such an important feature of Baxter's process.

For today's collector, the apparent scarcity of Baxter prints is something of a mystery, particularly as he claimed runs in excess of 700,000 for some of his more popular subjects. Certainly, a great many were used to decorate the scrapbooks of the Victorian period and this accounts for the high prices many of these now command at auction. Some of his large prints which include *The Day before Marriage* and *The Bridesmaid* are very scarce, as also are the popular oval series later re-published by Le Blond, but which somehow appear to lack the original Baxter magic.

Present custodians of Baxter prints should ensure that they are not hung where they can be subjected to direct sunlight or fading will certainly result. For those who own them they represent a premium investment in the pleasure and interest they provide.

No. 26 Print from Baxter type oval key-plate—aquatint *Author's Collection*

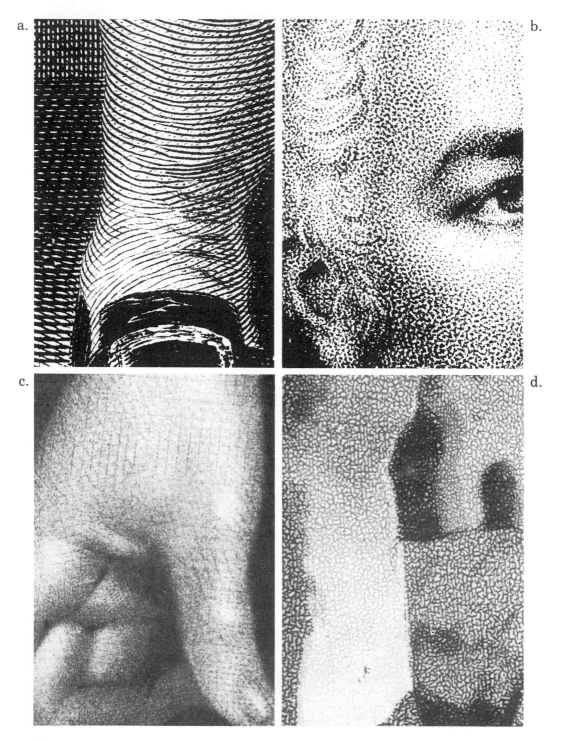

a.

b.

c.

d.

Notes on Baxter prints

Unique colour printing process developed by George Baxter in mid-Victorian period combining both intaglio and relief printing.

The use of oil based inks provided brilliant colour contrasts.

Several unsuccessful attempts made by competitors to match Baxter quality, including Leighton and Knight.

Prints representative of most aspects of life in Victorian Britain.

Baxter prints in good unfaded condition are now scarce, particularly large items and ovals.

A great many forgeries in early 20th century which may be recognised by screen pattern (dots) on prints.

Prints should not be hung in direct sunlight.

The inclusion of Baxter prints in some Victorian scrapbooks contribute to their high prices in the salerooms.

Of the numbers claimed by Baxter to have been produced, their scarcity when compared with other prints of the period (e.g. topographical line engravings) is difficult to understand.

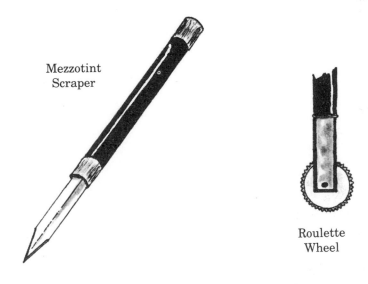

Mezzotint
Scraper

Roulette
Wheel

No. 27 (*opposite page*) Enlargements of print making techniques a)line engraving; b)stipple; c)mezzotint; d)aquatint

71

Print
Collecting

Print Collecting

Collecting is a matter of personal taste, closely allied to one's knowledge, enthusiasm, financial resources and the availability of the items sought. One of the delights of all collecting is the unexpected find which sometimes enables the experienced collector to acquire a rare and important item at a fraction of its market value.

Some years ago I was offered an unusual book of star-charts by a reputable bookseller who had been unable to trace the item in *Book Auction Records* (see note on Research and Reference) as the work was without title page or publisher's imprint. The book had been sewn into soft covers, now much battered and worn, but the contents revealed a series of superb copper-plate engravings; bright crisp impressions, clearly an early printing from the plates. From the position of the plate-marks a date somewhere between 1700 and 1760 suggested itself. An offer of what was then considered to be of generous proportions was made and accepted.

Subsequent research involved correspondence with the British Museum, the Greenwich Observatory and finally the Royal Astronomical Society. This was followed by a visit to the Map Room of the British Museum where the item was confirmed as one of a limited number of proof copies of a rare star-atlas. It had been printed and issued only weeks before bankruptcy proceedings had closed the firm back in 1750. A court order had decreed the destruction of all the copper-plates used in its preparation. It now seems likely that there are less than twenty surviving copies of this rare unpublished work still in existence. (See *Proceedings of the American Philosophical Society, Vol. 125, No. 1, February, 1981.*)

The newcomer to print collecting will quickly realise that a working knowlege of old prints is not something that can be acquired overnight, for the scope of the subject is enormous. There is a very real need to specialise, for a collection based on a theme is likely to be more interesting and also more valuable than an haphazard selection. There are great areas of interest at prices to suit all pockets. Many of the delightful topographical steel engravings of the last century can still be bought at prices lower than the cost of some modern reproductions!

Old prints were originally published in the books of the period, issued in sets (e.g. Sporting prints) or sold as individual items. In general terms the former source is more common but, if of comparative quality, the latter are more likely to be sought by the discriminating collector. This is not to suggest that rare and valuable prints do not appear in books; many of the fine aquatint plate books of the last century are now very scarce and quite beyond the reach of the modest collector.

Where to see old prints

The important national collections are housed at the British Museum, the Victoria and Albert Museum and the National Maritime Museum at Greenwich. In addition, some local authorities have their own museums and art galleries displaying items of local or county interest. Many people derive great pleasure from visiting exhibitions without any thought of becoming collectors. Even as this is being written there is a breathtaking exhibition on the work of Wenzel Hollar at the British Museum.

Exhibitions have a particular value for serious print collectors as they provide an opportunity to see and evaluate the items and, perhaps, compare these with similar examples owned by themselves. There is an unfortunate misconception held by many people that because books written about collecting often carry illustrations reproduced by courtesy of a particular museum, any similar examples will be in museums!

Whilst it is true that there is a great wealth of printed illustration housed in our national institutions, there are also a great many private collections and items from these are often loaned for exhibitions. Many unique art finds continue to be discovered by specialist collectors and dealers. The popular BBC television programme on antiques has created great public interest in collecting and has had its share of important and valuable 'finds'.

Intending collectors should regularly visit print-dealers noting the prices, range and quality of the prints on offer. Many dealers issue catalogues of their stock. Some of these are elaborate publications, extensively illustrated and inclined to be costly, but their acquisition should form part of the essential background research of the serious collector.

It is not recommended practice to visit print dealers premises and start searching through drawers or portfolios without first having the courtesy to introduce oneself and declare an interest. All prints should be handled with reverence and care.

The experienced dealer can tell at a glance by the way a client handles his stock whether he is dealing with a collector or a vandal! Apart from the framed prints displayed on his walls, the bulk of a dealer's stock will be stored in portfolios. These will be brought on request, the client being left to browse at his leisure. Each print should be carefully examined, a note being made of quality and condition. Holding an item to the light may reveal a watermark in the paper and often provide evidence of an early, or late impression. After inspection each print should be placed carefully face-down on the opposite board of the portfolio. Many dealers prefer to close and tie their own portfolios after clients have finished with them.

How prints are classified

Prints may be classified as follows; (a) original issues, (b) re-issues, (c) re-strikes, (d) reproductions, (e) copies made with intent to defraud, i.e. forgeries or fakes.

An original or early issue indicates an example taken from a first printing of the plate after various proof copies have been pulled. A re-issue may have been printed several years after the original printing and may or may not carry the imprint of the original publisher. Quite obviously, the earlier the impression the better, particularly as far as copper-plate examples are concerned.

The aquatint of *Lord Howe's Victory* (Plate 53), is one of several in the collection that came from a copy of *Jenkins Naval Achievements* published in 1817. On holding the print to the light a Whatman watermark dated 1821 is revealed, conclusive proof that this item could not have been printed as part of the first edition of the book. This particular re-issue appears to have lost none of the fine engraving in the sky and a very experienced eye would be needed to pronounce that a similar framed example was not an original issue! The writer bought a copy of *Jenkin's Naval Achievements* some ten or so years ago for several hundred pounds but its price today would be several thousand. The plates are somewhat small and thirty years ago would not really have attracted the serious collector of maritime prints.

The expression *re-strike* is normally used to indicate a modern impression taken from an original hand-worked plate. Many old copper plates have been provided with a soft steel surface to improve their wearing qualities and this can be renewed as soon as the steel starts to break down. Re-strikes carry the skill of the original engraver (for this same plate was used to produce the much sought after early impressions) but paper and printing are modern. Whilst it must be stated that re-strikes are works of art, they tend not to find favour with serious collectors.

Reproductions are usually modern copies produced by taking photographs of old prints from which the printing plates are then made. To be legal these examples should carry the imprint of the publisher and the date of publication. A great many small topographical prints of the last century are now being produced in this way. In the Midlands recently the author saw some Simkin military prints (chromo-lithographs) that had been reproduced in colour with the 'dot' tell-tale pattern but were complete with stickers claiming that they were over one hundred years old!

Back in 1894 the famous publisher's Raphael Tuck and Sons produced two attractive chromo-lithographs of the Liverpool and Manchester Railway based on the earlier work of John Shaw. Similar designs were used on postage stamps commemorating the one hundred and fiftieth anniversary of the opening of the Liverpool and Manchester Railway, a year or so ago. These prints are now collector's items and nine years hence will see them take their place in the collection as antiques. The day would therefore seem to be not too distant when we shall be able to enjoy genuine antique reproductions—perish the thought!

Fraudulent prints

The fraudulent production of old master prints is a practice nearly as old as the prints themselves and, fortunately, does not concern us here. From the standpoint of popular print collecting modern lithography is the process that has unwittingly aided the forger. Provided an original monochrome print is available to photograph, a half-tone screen is not needed and the give away 'dot' pattern on the print will be absent. Many such examples appeared on the market at the turn of the century and were produced on thick soft paper, already yellowed with age even before printing commenced!

The famous series of *London Cries* by Thomas Rowlandson met with a popular response, possibly beaten into second place by Francis Wheatley's thirteen plates on the *Cries of London*. Many of Morland's subjects were also forged. Comparisons may be difficult for the new collector but a study of the fine colour printed mezzotints and stipples in the Print Room of the British Museum will ensure that hand-coloured copies are readily recognised.

It is unlikely that any of these deceptions were ever bought by serious print collectors. Then as now, they find their way onto the market via the small country salerooms, suitably aged and residing in battered frames, their backs doubtless sealed with an old pasted newspaper bearing a turn of the century date! Small wonder the majority of collectors a century ago relied on the services of the professional print-dealer. This very day I was asked to comment on a set of Alken sporting prints bought recently in Wales. They are reproduced in black and white from Sutherland's aquatints and carry the familiar dotted pattern of the modern half-tone lithographic process. Heavy hand-colouring, badly executed, convinced the buyer they were old and he thought they were a bargain at thirty pounds apiece! By great good fortune two prints from this set of three hang in our dining room but, regretfully, the comparison only added insult to injury.

How to look at prints

Old prints cannot be inspected in detail without the aid of a good magnifying glass, possibly an x2 for normal use and an x20 (a type used by stamp collectors) for close and detailed examination. The reader can practice with the powerful glass on a known line engraving by making a comparison between the cut lines on this and the 'fuzzy' detail that will be evident on lithographs and reproductions.

You may have noticed that all the prints in the main section of the book carry dimensions with the height given first. Measurements are given to the edges of the engraved surface. Print measurement is a habit that should be cultivated and was the means of the writer detecting some clever lithographic forgeries of important yachts that were issued earlier this century. The original plates are quite large, but the fraudulent copies were some two inches smaller than they should have been.

The terms 'landscape' and 'portrait' may confuse the new collector because these expressions have nothing to do with the actual detail of a particular painting or print.

Landscape simply means that an item when viewed is longer than it is high and Portrait that the item has greater height than width. The aquatint of the *Stone Cross at Rouen* (illustrated) is an example of portrait landscape.

Paper, handling and inspection

Great care is necessary when handling unframed items and touching the engraved surface should be avoided, except when testing for ink deposits in dark areas of an engraving where photographic reproduction is suspected. Holding an item up to the light will reveal possible watermarks and also whether a *laid* or *wove* paper has been used. Laid papers carry lines at regular intervals usually about one inch apart. These were caused by the moisture attraction of the wire trays used to support the wet paper during making. Papermakers took advantage of this discovery and built designs into the bottom of their trays made from soldered wire. All kinds of devices were used, and in both Britain and France during the 18th century the date of manufacture was sometimes incorporated into the design. Certain emblems became so well known that some paper sizes were named after them, like crown and foolscap. The Fool's-cap was introduced by the early British paper maker Sir John Spielman in the late 16th century.

Wove paper first made its appearance in the nineteenth century when the method of manufacture was changed and wire-marks disappeared, although watermarks were still retained. These later papers tend to be heavier and better quality than much of the paper used in previous centuries. All old paper in original condition is highly absorbent and designed deliberately to attract ink at the printing stage. A moistened little finger applied to a paper margin will prove the point unless the paper has been previously sized for colouring or is of modern origin. Apart from the presence of watermarks and the type of paper used, holding an item up to the light will often reveal whether a print has been damaged and subsequently repaired. On the print of *The Glutton* in the collection, new margins (the paper border surrounding the print) had been added and were only detected when the item was removed from the frame. The work had been skillfully carried out and it was only when the print was turned face down that evidence of folding was noticed which did not extend into the margins. Sadly, there are very few restorers whom one could find today to undertake restoration work to this standard.

Trends in collecting

It is interesting to look back at the books on print collecting that were published in the early years of the present century and compare collecting trends then, with those of today. A century ago the province of the print collector was very much a question of taste, wealth and leisure and there was little if any opportunity to develop the former without the compensations of the latter.

It had become fashionable to collect mezzotints. Prices rose rapidly with the increasing public interest in the colour-printed examples of the previous century. A cultured and wealthy minority concerned itself with

80

the pursuit of old master prints and coupled this with an almost obsessional desire for early 'states' and impressions.

The slump conditions following the First World War resulted in panic selling and many prints returned to the salerooms to become part of the glut of seemingly over-priced and unwanted art, for fashion in art may become a dangerous bedfellow. It seems, however, that the majority of old master prints stayed where they were, a continuing source of interest and pleasure to their fortunate owners.

Between wars, the interest in old prints appears to have waned somewhat, one York bookseller in the 1930's using his stock of large Buck panoramic views as wrapping material for his books. At today's prices this exercise would cost him at least two hundred and fifty pounds per parcel!

Many of the prints now sought by today's collector are not mentioned by Whitman or Hayden, although a general lack of interest in mezzotint portraits is understandable.

There is, however, a great demand for sporting and coaching items and for early railway and marine prints as well as large topographical views in aquatint and lithography. The discerning collector appears to entertain little interest for today's costly mass-produced 'limited edition', where the pencilled signature on a Russell Flint or Lowrie print sometimes attracts a price-tag that would have bought the original painting!

Today, an original Dutton 'shipper' or an early Pollard 'coacher' is unlikely to be ousted by a new generation of either—they simply do not make them anymore!

Print conservation—cleaning

The paper on which old prints were printed was highly absorbent to attract ink at the printing stage. This makes it particularly susceptible to moisture. Prints that have been stored or hung in damp surroundings will attract moisture and may become spotted or stained. This unsightly staining is known as 'foxing' and without treatment the paper in the affected areas is likely to rot. There is also a condition known as 'iron mould', which produces reddish brown spots and is caused by the mineral impurities present in some early papers.

It is possible to remove 'foxing' by washing prints in a mixture of domestic bleach and water. However, attempting to clean valuable prints without first obtaining practical experience in the cleaning process is foolish in the extreme. The suggestion is to first attempt cleaning by buying a number of insignificant and inexpensive prints. Some print-dealers offer bargain bundles suitable for this purpose. Very little equipment is needed apart from a couple of developing trays of suitable size and plenty of blotting paper. The trays can be bought from most photographic shops and are quite inexpensive.

One tray is filled with clean water and the other is used for the bleach. It is necessary to be able to move prints from one tray to the other without handling them. A piece of perspex or thin sheet aluminium should be cut to fit the bottom of the tray. This carrier should not be a tight fit, otherwise it will be impossible to slide the fingers down the side of the tray in order to lift it out. I use picture glass, having first bound the edges with waterproof tape. Wet glass is, however, very slippery and could be dangerous if used by the inexperienced.

Proceed as follows: Place the carrier in the bottom of the tray containing clean water and pop the print to be cleaned into the tray, allowing it to soak for several minutes. This preliminary soaking is necessary because the foxed areas on the print have already absorbed considerable moisture and the bleaching solution would react more quickly on these than on the surrounding areas of the print. Failure to observe this simple advice may result in a cleaned print having white spots instead of brown, although I see modern reproductions are now appearing on the market complete with foxing!

A mixture of twenty per cent bleach in water ought not be exceeded, i.e. one measure by volume of bleach to four measures of water. The size of the measuring container will depend on the size of the tray used, although a solution depth of about one inch is usually sufficient for prints up to folio size.

The print is now carefully raised on the carrier, allowing the surplus water to drain off before transfer to the bleaching tray, where carrier and print are gently allowed to submerge. As soon as the foxing disappears, the print should be lifted out, drained, and carefully returned to the clean water and left to soak for at least ten minutes to remove all traces of bleach. This part of the process is most important and soaking times must not be reduced.

The print is then raised on the carrier, drained, and placed on a flat working surface. Ample supplies of white blotting paper are essential. Use one piece to gently press over the surface area of the print to remove any excess moisture. A second piece should be gently pressed down over the print and then print and carrier are carefully turned over onto the working surface enabling the carrier to be liberated, leaving the print to dry. No form of heat (hair-dryers and the like) should be used in an attempt to accelerate the drying time, otherwise the print will 'cockle' causing the paper to ripple and its appearance will be marred.

With experience, it may be possible to dispense with carriers for prints that have been printed on fairly heavy paper, popping them in and out of the trays by holding them by their corners. This should not be attempted with either large or valuable items. Do ensure that the clean water tray is changed regularly and contains as much water as possible.

Prints on India paper

At a recent London print sale some copies of Finden's *Ports and Harbours* did not reach the price expected, despite a strong dealer presence. Finden's is a delightful two volume work with steel engravings of British seaports and there is a constant demand for the prints, particularly the volume containing shipping scenes after Edward William Cooke. The prints in question were spotted or foxed and had been printed on India paper, a process which prevents bleach washing.

India paper is a very fine, soft paper that was usually reserved for early impressions from a plate. This was first stuck to the surface of a backing paper before printing and a very experienced eye is needed to detect its presence. Due to impurities in the paste used to stick them to the backing paper, many prints on India paper are likely to be found in a spotted condition. They could be cleaned by means of a fume cupboard but this process is expensive. If an attempt is made to clean them by the method I have described, the India paper carrying the impression will float off and lie on the surface of the water! Prints in this state have little chance of ever being returned to their former condition.

Laid-down prints

When a print has been stuck to a card backing it is said to have been 'laid down'. There are several possible reasons why this practice may have been resorted to and all should be regarded with suspicion. Prints that have been torn or otherwise damaged may have been laid down in order to preserve a valuable item that might otherwise have had to be discarded, and this is quite acceptable. The modern restorer usually uses a backing that is light enough to reveal the damage when the item is raised to the light. However, a heavy card back was often used in the last century so that both damage and watermark were hidden. Fake items were often treated in this way and prevent a thorough examination of the paper on which they are printed.

It is not possible to clean prints that have been laid down without first soaking off the backing. They should be immersed in clean hot water. I use four stainless steel forks placed on the backboard to provide sufficient weight to keep the item submerged. The water should be regularly changed and the print checked from time to time to see whether it is starting to release itself from the backing. The condition of prints is not improved by constant soaking and it is sometimes necessary to pick off the back, a somewhat skilled and painstaking operation. Never on any account attempt to pull a print away from its backing; work in the reverse manner pulling the backing away from the print.

When the print is finally released it may be cleaned in the manner previously described. After cleaning, ensure it is placed face down on the blotting paper, otherwise on the following day you may find it has a new back by being stuck to the blotting paper!

Print colouring and sizing

When hand coloured prints are cleaned there is usually a loss of colour and re-colouring becomes necessary. However, prints that have been printed in colour by the intaglio process are unlikely to be affected by cleaning. Some late Victorian chromo-lithographs tend to lose colour as do some Baxter-type prints. It is unwise to attempt to clean Baxter's using more than a ten per cent bleach application and the prints should be removed from the cleaning fluid as soon as the foxing begins to fade.

Many old prints were sized before they were hand coloured. This greatly reduced the high absorption properties of paper. It is possible for a skilled colourist to hand colour on un-sized paper but this is not recommended. The sizing process puts a fine glue-like film on the paper and prevents the water colour spreading. Hand colouring on unsized paper is not unlike attempting to apply watercolour to blotting paper!

The glue size recommended has tended to be replaced by modern paste but it is still available from certain ironmongers and shops selling decorating materials. The size is in crystal form and should be mixed according to the instructions on the packet. I use a half teaspoonful of size to a mug of water and this should prove sufficient to size at least a dozen fairly large prints. A small quantity of boiling water should be used to dissolve the crystals, topped up with cold water, after which sizing may commence.

The print to be sized is placed face down on a piece of glass or on some other suitable dry and smooth working surface. It is important to work quickly and a soft clean paint brush with a width of at least two inches should be used. Brushing should be in one direction only. By stopping short of the outer edges of the print the item may be handled without difficulty. The size will be quickly absorbed by the paper and re-brushing should be avoided.

The prints may be clipped on an indoor line to dry or placed face down on a piece of blanket material. A drying time of at least twenty-four hours should be allowed before hand colouring is attempted.

Print colouring

Today's colourist will normally use good quality tube watercolours although some perfectionists still manage to find old Victorian colourist's boxes. These often contain stick-colours which I keep for work on valuable or important items.

It is possible to buy uncoloured reproductions of old prints and maps (see list of dealers) and these provide a basis for developing ones artistic skills before more serious work on antique items is attempted. Newcomers to hand colouring are usually surprised at the speed with which they become proficient and the pleasure they derive from the activity naturally increases as confidence grows.

Print care and repair

Thanks to modern technology there is now a very extensive range of products available to the restorer and the archivist and some of these can be safely used by practical print collectors. Torn prints can be skillfully repaired by using a special paper which is applied by means of a hot iron, after the removal of a backing paper. The material looks very much like tissue paper but is immensely strong. It will accept watercolour and is almost invisible when applied. It is one of a range of products made by Archival Aids, Ademco Ltd., of Coronation Road, Cressex Estate, High Wycombe, Buckinghamshire, who would doubtless provide the addresses of local stockists.

If old prints are to continue to outlive their owners, some thought ought to be given to their ongoing care. Frequently, they are hung above open fireplaces or over radiators where localised heat will dry out the paper to such an extent that it will become brittle. This deterioration will not be evident until an attempt is made to remove the item from its frame. Central heating may be excellent for humans but room temperatures in excess of 60 degrees Farenheit are bad for old prints. Producing this book has meant that a great many of my prints have had to be removed from their frames for reproduction purposes; all are now to be backed with archival tissue before being re-hung.

Prints ought to be framed in such a way that they cannot come into direct contact with the glass of the picture. This can be overcome by inserting the print into a card window mount of suitable thickness. The picture-framer of a century ago had perhaps a rather better idea. He inserted a gilt slip between the item and the glass, thus ensuring the essential passage of air over the surface of the print. This slip material can still be purchased from discerning picture framers.

Records

The dedicated collector may be in some difficulty with the detailed recording of his purchases, especially if he has a wife who feels that the money would have been better spent on a new carpet! As a young man I worked for some years for a country solicitor. The death of a client would result in inventories being produced that had to be carefully checked against house contents and these often included small antique items of great value.

Perhaps we ought to share with the nobility and gentry their sensible concern for recording these details of their goods and chattels. When we have done this with our prints we may possibly think it worthwhile to extend the arrangement to the rest of our possessions.

A boxed card index may be bought from most stationers for very little, but a couple of packs of postcards and a few rubber bands will serve equally well. Individual columns will record the date of purchase, the title and size of the item, the buying source and the price paid. A receipt is essential, even when buying from relatives.

A few weeks ago, a near neighbour with a great love for antiques had a visit from a valuer employed by one of the famous London auction houses. She was astonished to learn that a relatively modern watercolour she had bought from a near relative for a small sum, some fifteen years ago, was worth something in excess of ten thousand pounds. Imagine her distress when she related the news to the relative concerned only to be told that he had merely loaned her the picture in the first place; whereupon he promptly departed, taking the painting with him!

Not surprisingly, many antique items, including maps and prints have enjoyed marked appreciation over the years. Their increasing rarity is now unlikely to suffer from any changes in collecting fashion. There is, for example, little chance of a fine Dutton maritime lithograph or an early Pollard coaching print ever forming part of a future collecting 'trend', for fashion dictates the need for a sufficient supply of a particular commodity to generate popular demand. The experienced collector seeks interest and quality within the field of his special interest and, hopefully, is able to make a value judgement on a particular item before the next man gets to it!

Security

The seemingly wholesale theft of valuable antiques and works of art continues to increase at an alarming rate and many people are finding it necessary to arrange additional security in their homes, usually by providing extra locking devices on doors and windows. There appears little likelihood of any improvement in this state of affairs within our present society. The advice given in *Looking at Old Maps* about the value of security marking is clearly being heeded by many collectors. What is the point in providing the Police with a photograph of a stolen item without the information of some special distinguishing mark that will enable it to be readily identified?

Most security firms supply the American *Volumatic* marker pen which enables a collector to write his name across an item with what amounts to invisible ink. There is no possibility of damage to the print and identification can immediately be established by the use of ultra-violet scanning equipment that is in increasing use by the police.

Insurance provision

Readers will be surprised to learn that a valuable collection of old prints may not be covered under the terms of the 'contents' insurance on their homes, particularly if any one item has a value in excess of a hundred pounds. Special insurance of this kind is not cheap but neither is the theft and subsequent loss of treasured possessions. A proper listing of the collection with regular up-dating as to values will greatly assist your insurance company or broker to advise on the type of cover needed.

Let the buyer beware

Since the publication of the previous book on map collecting, several dealers and private individuals have expressed appreciation for the information it contained about the legality of buying from unknown sources. The advice is repeated here with the print collector in mind.

Collectors and dealers often buy from each other and from private individuals. Both need to be especially careful when making purchases from unknown third parties. There are both dealers and collectors who have cause to regret certain 'good buys' that later turned into 'goodbyes' because they had unwittingly bought stolen property. If you are in the least doubtful about an intended purchase, particularly if the price appears to be on the low side, or if cash is insisted upon 'because of the tax-man,' you would be well advised not to buy.

When dealing with strangers always ask for a receipt incorporating a statement that the goods are the seller's own unencumbered property and that they are prepared to indemnify you against any claims arising out of the purchase. The name and address of the seller should be witnessed by the signature of a third party (not his wife). This information may be requested in all good faith and if a seller takes umbridge, so be it. At least there will be no future likelihood of your being charged with 'receiving', should your purchase turn out to have been previously stolen. Reputable dealers continue to be caught in a trap arising from a chain reaction involving the reputable dealer, who buys from another reputable dealer, who bought from a doubtful source, who in turn bought from a thief!

Aids to research and reference

For many print enthusiasts this aspect of collecting is probably the most interesting and rewarding. The serious collector can never have too many research aids available to him but, unlike Roy Plomley's castaways on *Desert Island Discs* (BBC Radio), a single book on the subject can do little more than highlight some of the obvious aspects of the interest. Suitable reference books are an essential part of the print collector's armoury and these may well enable him to compete with the professional dealer with his knowledge of the subject and in the auction room. All reference books should, however, be regarded with a certain amount of reservation for it is not uncommon to find one author's errors (as well as his discoveries) perpetuated by other writers in the same field!

One of the most useful books for the intending print collector is Herbert Slater's monumental work *Engravings and Their Value*. This was first published in the late 19th century and by 1921 had reached its Fifth Edition, which rather suggests that print collecting was as popular then as now. The book runs to well over seven hundred pages and commences with an explanation of the various print making processes and goes on to list many hundreds of engravers, together with details of their works, dating from the earliest times to the middle of the last century. As a price guide it is, of course, hopelessly out of date but nevertheless provides interesting, if sometimes dubious, assessments on the abilities of some engravers. By way of example, Charles Eden Wagstaff who engraved *The Wedding of Queen Victoria* (Plate 61) is described as 'An engraver in line whose name is associated with a large variety of well known but for the most part unimportant prints, which being at the time very popular were issued in large numbers. Their present value, with few exceptions is small, and in some cases quite trifling'.

Another book much used and prized by collectors and dealers is *A Dictionary of Artists* by Algernon Graves F.S.A., first published in 1884 and subsequently revised and updated at the turn of the century. This formidable work lists some sixteen thousand artists and engravers working in Britain for 1760 onwards. It gives details of their specialist painting or engraving interest, where they lived and the names of the various institutions and galleries where their works were exhibited. A reference to J. M. W. Turner R.A. lists his specialist interest as *Landscape* and credits him with two hundred and fifty-nine exhibitions at the Royal Academy. This particular book has been a great practical value to me on many occasions by helping to establish that the name on a picture or print by an apparently unknown artist or engraver was that of an important worker in his field.

A more recent reference work of great value to print collectors is *Book Auction Records*, published annually by Messrs William Dawson and Sons Ltd., of Folkestone, Kent. This lists all the important printed books sold at auctions in the previous year by the major British auction houses. The book not only provides a price guide of books sold (generally regarded as a trade price for the works concerned) but also lists useful additional information as to date of original publication, together with the names of the author and/or artists concerned, the number of illustrations and details of watermarks. A dedicated researcher with, say, a ten year run of this trade 'bible' could doubtless compile a comprehensive bibliography on most of the important plate-books that have been produced from Caxton's time to the middle of the last century, many of which contain the old prints sought by today's collector.

A little serious research of *Book Auction Records* will provide interesting evidence of collecting trends and price movements. A glance at a 1970/1 edition lists only one sale of the rare book *Jenkins Naval Achievements* (see plate 53) during that year. The price paid was £540 and represented ten pounds each for the fifty-four maritime aquatints it contained. In 1978/9 a comparable copy sold for £2,300, a unit price per plate of something over forty pounds each. In other words, the prints had quadrupled in price in eight years at dealers 'buying in' price. This very considerable rise was doubtless due in part to inflation but the price also reflects the increasing scarcity surrounding works of art of this kind.

It is likely that many of the larger library authorities will carry copies of these various books in their reference sections but none are likely to be available on the usual public loan. This arrangement dictates that research will have to be undertaken in the library building itself and this may not always be convenient. Nevertheless, the high cost of acquiring reference works of this kind places a serious custodial responsibility on library authorities, who are normally only too anxious to make their resources available to as wide a readership as possible.

Some secondhand booksellers specialise in art reference books and it is worth inspecting their stock and leaving details of ones requirements. Many issue catalogues from time to time and are only too willing to add the name of a serious customer to their mailing list. There are also regular sales of secondhand books arranged by most of the provincial auction houses, where books on collecting may often be bought under the hammer at very realistic prices. Perhaps it should be pointed out that the books listed in *Book Auction Records* are mostly rare and valuable items and any reference works quoted are likely to be somewhat specialised and expensive.

For the reader interested in sporting prints, the late Captain Siltzer's book *The Story of British Sporting Prints* is a most useful work. In the 18th and 19th century it was not uncommon for a painting by a particular artist to be engraved by several different engravers. One example might be produced by the mezzotint process, another by line engraving, whilst a third could well be lithographed. The information on the engraver, publisher and date of publication are all points of reference that need to be checked. In the Siltzer book there are a great many technical errors with regard to the print processes employed. Without a copy of the print to hand, the task of making corrections is very difficult. I revised my copy of the book, correcting some twenty errors regarding processes and then ran out of prints!

Some years ago I bought a fine pair of sporting engravings by Edward Hacker—*Will Long on Bertha* and *Charles Davis on The Traverser*, after paintings by Barraud brothers William and Henry. Will Long was Whip to the Duke of Beaufort and Charles Davis was the Royal huntsman at Windsor and brother of R. B. Davis the sporting artist. Both prints were line engraved by Edward Hacker (1813–1905) who also produced a

90

number of prints for the *Sporting Magazine*. I was shocked to find that they were classified by Siltzer as mezzotints. There was evidence on the flanks of *The Traverser* that might be rocker work but was more likely evidence of roulette wheel work. The prints were signed in pencil by both artists and had doubtless been presented to some patron. I was interested to read the imprint 'Published by the Artists' because I had seen both before where the publisher was given as James Sheldon of 31, Ely Place. This new information indicated that the prints were first published by the Barrauds themselves and any impressions found with Sheldon's name on them must be later re-prints.

A visit to London was made with *Traverser* and *Bertha* and an audience duly granted at a certain venerable institution. Could they please say which print-making process had been used to make the prints? A charming young man promptly disappeared and returned clutching a copy of *Siltzer*. 'They are mezzotints' he proudly announced; deep breath by amateur collector—'I think they are line engravings'; hasty exit by young man who returns with white-haired academic looking gentleman whom one instinctively felt knew his business. 'They are line engravings' announced venerable gentleman. 'But Sir, Captain Siltzer says they are mezzotints' said the young man with signs of despair. 'Well Captain Siltzer is wrong. Cross out the entry in pencil and insert line engraving', said the venerable gentleman and promptly dissapeared, no doubt to concentrate on matters of much greater importance.

Each year both the British Museum, the Victoria and Albert Museum and the National Maritime Museum answer literally thousands of letters and enquiries from all over the world about prints. Often the information supplied is insufficient to enable any positive identification to be made. The size of the engraved surface should be quoted, the title, details of the artist and engraver and the date of publication. Better still, a photograph of the item can be of considerable help. Do not expect any of these institutions to provide a valuation, for they are not permitted to express opinions as to the value of the items submitted. The major auction houses are usually prepared to evaluate 'finds' based on their considerable experience in selling items of this kind.

The reader may have read in a previous chapter that I have classified all old prints as either *original* or *interpretive* and I hasten to add that this classification is not shared by all writers on the subject. May I support my point by saying that I regard Hollar's shipping print (Plate 8) and Sandby's *Worcester* (Plate 33) as *original* prints because both men conceived the respective designs and executed the work on the printing plates. By contrast, the example by David Lucas of *The Lock* (Plate 57) was his interpretation in mezzotint of an original painting by John Constable.

Today's informed collector will naturally place a higher premium on a work that was executed by a known master than he will on a copy etched, engraved or lithographed by someone after that master's work. Although this point may appear obvious, I am certainly grateful to those dealers who in the past enabled me to buy the original lithographs of Cooper, Harding and others without apparently appreciating their value and importance as *original* works of art.

A glance at many of the *interpretive* prints in the book will usually reveal two names on the print—artist and engraver. Normally that of the artist appears on the left below the lower margin, whilst the name of the engraver appears on the right. Both are usually supported by the title of the print and the name and address of the publisher. We have already seen how the name of the publisher can be helpful in determining whether the item is a first issue. This practice of inserting the names of artist and engraver arose from the artist signing the engraver's proof copies of the print made from his drawing or painting, to indicate that he considered the work a satisfactory and faithful rendering of his original.

The engraver signed on the right hand side and the printer typeset or had the engraver insert the two names by engraving them on the plate. Although this practice was widespread, it is surprising how many prints were published with incorrect spellings as far as engravers names were concerned. The great etcher Whistler continued this practice by signing his work in pencil beneath the print as proof that he had personally prepared the etching or lithograph concerned. This, alas, is quite different from today's artist, who often signs a mechanically produced copy of his original work taken from a printing plate that has been made by a photographic process.

Modern re-prints and reproductions

Many of the illustrated plate books of the last century are now being printed in modern form including Rowlandson's famous book on the *London Volunteers*, Howitt's *Field Sports*, Thomas Shotter Boys *London as it Is*, and many more. Often items from these books appear as framed prints in the auction rooms but the reader who has read the section of this book on Print Making Processes will readily recognise them for what they are, because of the 'dotted' composition of the colour plates.

Alken's famous *National Sports of Great Britain* was reproduced by chromo-lithography by Methuen in 1903 and has now become a valuable book. The plates are without the familiar 'dot' pattern and are sometimes passed off as being from the original 1821 edition that were, of course, aquatints and are much more valuable. Sound advice to the newcomer to collecting would be to first do a great deal of looking at prints in museums, print shops and in the various auction rooms where these items are regularly sold.

The readers expertise in this field will be matched by the amount of time and interest devoted to the subject. Those prints illustrated merely provide a glimpse of a fascinating and rewarding hobby and are by no means representative of the interest as a whole. The many omissions include Sam Howitt, the sporting painter and etcher, the prints after Landseer's animal studies, the Holy Land views of David Roberts, the fine aquatints of Thomas Malton and many, many more. There are a great number of fine and interesting prints that I do not possess and I have no doubt that in writing this book I have unwittingly reduced my chances of ever finding them!

'Many an amateur, by devoting his activities to one section, has acquired a greater knowledge of his subject than professionals trying to cover a wide field.'

F.L. Wilder

(*How to Identify Old Prints*)

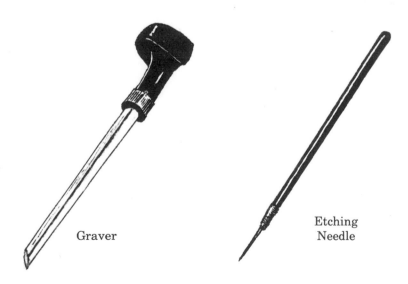

Graver

Etching
Needle

Prints and
Printmakers

Cornelius Caukercken fl. 1650

This copper engraving of King Charles II was engraved at Antwerp in 1658 by Cornelius Caukercken and was one of the plates used to illustrate the Duke of Newcastle's treatise on Horsemanship.

The Duke (1592–1676) was the King's (Charles I) luckless military commander in the north of England. On the 30th November, 1642 he marched south at the request of the Yorkshire royalists with six thousand horse and foot and seized the castle at Cawood (Plate 18) but was displaced by roundhead forces. The ultimate defeat of the royalists at the battle of Marston Moor in 1644 forced him to flee abroad. It was during this period of exile that he established the famous riding school to which the prints in this series relate.

His training techniques were based on a real desire to understand the mind and emotions of the horse and he combined this with the minimal use of the whip and physical punishment '... by mixing gentleness with help and corrections'. Several of the engravings in the book have English backgrounds of great interest, including Welbeck, Bolsover and Bothel Castle. The one illustrated depicts King Charles II in full armour with old London Bridge and the City in the background; overhead a cluster of angels bear the crowns of the four kingdoms, England, Scotland, Ireland and Wales.

The original edition was illustrated with forty-three copper plate engravings, some fifty woodcuts and printed in French. An English edition appeared in 1743 published by James Brindley, entitled *New Method of Horsemanship* and employed the original copper plates made three-quarters of a century before. All editions are now scarce and costly, although individual plates appear in the salerooms from time to time.

The versatile Duke was able to return to Britain after the Restoration, bringing with him Abraham Diepenbeck who had prepared the drawings for the original work. Shaw Sparrow recounts (*British Sporting Artists*) how Diepenbeck made the Duke a sketch of a galloping battle-horse, showing the hind feet raised from the ground and the fore ones flexed but this up-dated method of depicting a running horse was not to be developed by artists until after the invention of photography some two centuries later.

Process: Copper line engraving

Size: $14\frac{3}{4}''\times 19\frac{5}{8}''$ (362 × 499mm)

Watermark: Fleur-de-lys (1743)

Source: John and Judith Head
Barn Book Supply 1968

No. 28 King Charles II by Cornelius Caukercken—line engraving *Author's Collection*

William Hogarth 1697–1746

This important painter, etcher and engraver was born in London in 1697 during the reign of William III. On leaving school William was apprenticed to a silversmith and taught the skills of engraving on metal and, possibly, the rudiments of etching. After completing his apprenticeship he attended the St. Martin's Lane Academy to improve his drawing ability. He set up in business as an ornamental engraver and quickly found his skills in demand as an engraver of illustrative plates. This early work possibly directed his attention to the potential market that existed for the print-maker although by this time he had achieved some success as a portrait painter in oils. He introduced a new aspect into British art by painting characteristic groups of figures that became known as 'conversation pieces'.

His first important work was a series of six oil paintings depicting *A Harlot's Progress,* although the example illustrated is taken from his best known work *Marriage à la mode* now in the National Gallery. The prints were engraved by three important line engravers, G. Scotin, B. Baron and R. F. Ravenet (although one of the plates is signed S. Ravenet). Some of Hogarth's early work was engraved by himself but he found it necessary to engage other engravers in order to meet the popular demand for the prints after his paintings. An interesting point about the 'Marriage' series is that the engravers reproduced them directly off the originals and so the prints all appear the wrong way round when compared with the oil paintings.

In 1822 Messrs Baldwin and Cradock re-issued the original plates that had been re-worked, in a large elephant folio volume titled *Works of Hogarth.* Thomas Cook, a pupil of Ravenet, also issued an edition of Hogarth's work in 1802 that was re-issued in 1822, the same year as the Heath edition previously mentioned. They were also reproduced in a smaller format in what is commonly known as the Trusler edition in the mid-nineteenth century. Some of the plates towards the end of this particular book are photographic copies in later editions and in these ink transfer will be evident on the pages facing the genuine engravings. These plates were engraved on steel but, of course, now qualify as antiques by virtue of age.

Despite their satirical and moralistic commentary on life in Georgian Britain, Hogarth's prints do not appear to be in great demand. The 'Election' plates are popular as are 'Beer Street' and 'Gin Lane'; reproductions of the latter are often to be seen in establishments selling the beverages concerned!

Process: Line engraving   Source: Tolley Gallery 1973

Size: 14″ × 17½″ (356 × 445mm)

Watermark: None

98

No. 29   Marriage-à-la-Mode after William Hogarth—line engraving *Author's Collection*

James Seymour 1702–1752

When George III established the Royal Academy in 1768 a number of important British artists were overlooked. Shaw Sparrow inclined to the view that Britain's habitual neglect of native art had turned many painters into life-long primitives as a consequence. James Seymour was one such artist.

The rise of the sporting print in Britain owes much of its popularity to the early sporting painters like John Wooton, George Stubbs, James Seymour and the Sartorius family. Among the early publishers who reproduced their paintings for the newly established print market of the 18th century were Carington Bowles and Robert Sayer.

Some years ago when visiting Aylesbury I had the good fortune to find in a bookshop a copy of Sayer's publication *Seymour's 12 Prints of Hunters and Running Horses Taken in Various Actions*. This is similar to a copy of the same work published by Carington Bowles. Both provide a valuable link between the Newcastle prints mentioned on a previous page and the sporting work of Henry Alken and his contemporaries in the early nineteenth century.

Seymour was self taught and, despite being the son of an important City banker, shared Morland's apparent dislike of the nobility and gentry. Shaw Sparrow records how the Duke of Somerset (whose family name was also Seymour) commissioned Seymour to decorate a room at Petworth with portraits of his race horses. The Duke treated Seymour as a guest but felt the painter arrogant and lacking in respect.

One day at dinner the Duke toasted Seymour with the comment 'Cousin Seymour your health!' to which Seymour replied 'My Lord, I really do believe that I have the honour of being of your Grace's family'. At this the Duke lost control of himself and left the room ordering his steward to dismiss the painter. Months later, with the work unfinished, the artist who had been engaged to complete Seymour's work begged to be excused as the work was beyond his capabilities and suggested to the Duke that Seymour be asked to complete it.

The summons to Petworth was answered by Seymour who upon hearing the Duke's request replied—'My Lord, I will now prove that I am of your Grace's family; for I won't come!'. And he never did.

Process: Copper Line engraving and etching

Source: Weatherheads Bookshop 1973

Size: 6″ × 10″ (152 × 250mm)

Watermark: None

Seymour's 12 Prints of Hunters and Running Horses. Taken in Various Actions.

No. 30   A Hunter taking a Flying Leap after James Seymour—copper line engraving *Author's Collection*

George Edwards 1694–1773 and John Gould 1804–81

One early pioneer in British ornithology was George Edwards, whose *Natural History of Uncommon Birds* (1743) and *Gleanings of Natural History* (1758) carry etched plates prepared by himself. The illustration of the Great Black Cockatoo is dated 1761 and doubtless appeared in the latter work published between 1758 and 1764. His drawings possess a certain primitive charm but are sometimes marred by poor hand colouring. It is only in recent years that the importance of Edward's work has been appreciated and evidence suggests that some were used as juvenile colouring books in the last century.

Edwards was for a time Librarian to the Royal College of Physicians, a post which enabled him to continue his researches. Often sailors returning from abroad would bring home parrots and other tropical species and Edwards hearing of a recent arrival would rush off with his sketch pad to make the necessary drawing. His careful draughtsmanship is evident on the Cockatoo, where he illustrates the bird's beak full size with the note, 'bigness of life'.

The researches of Edwards were dwarfed the following century by the work of John Gould and his wife. The Gould bird books were one of the great publishing successes of the 19th century and were produced entirely by lithography. The early printings were by Hullmandel, Britain's first lithographic printer. Many folios were hand coloured to a very high standard, the plummage being highlighted by the application of gum-arabic. The Goulds' first production was *A Century of Birds from the Himalaya Mountains* (80 plates), followed by *Birds of Europe* (488 plates). Between 1862 and 1873 they published *Birds of Great Britain* (367 plates). This was followed by two further works on toucans and the trogans. *Birds of Australia*, a mammoth work containing over six hundred different species, was followed by the monograph of *The Humming Birds* (418 plates). Gould died before this was completed and R. Bowdler Sharp continued with its publication and also *The Birds of Asia*.

The old established London booksellers Messrs Henry Sotheran Ltd., have specialised in the sale of Gould folios and prints for many years.

Process: Edwards etching, Source: Edwards—John Orde, 1983
       Gould lithograph   Gould—Tolley Gallery, 1970

Size: Edwards 12″ × 8½″ (305 × 216mm)
      Gould 24″ × 18″ (601 × 457mm) paper size

Watermarks: None

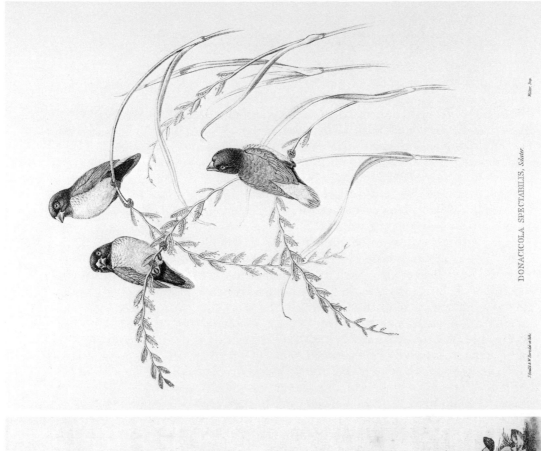

DONACICOLA SPECTABILIS, *Sclater.*

No. 31　Birds by George Edwards and John Gould—a)etching; b)lithograph *Author's Collection*

George 'Smith of Chichester' 1714–76

Although the work of the original etchers is rather outside the scope of this book, I have chosen to include one such example by the Smith brothers of Chichester, who were forerunners of the artist-etcher tradition. George Smith appears to have been a landscape artist of some merit and the famous engraver Woollett worked after him, perhaps giving his work an importance it might otherwise not have enjoyed. By the mid-eighteenth century the somewhat crude topographical work of the brothers Buck had helped to establish a tradition of topographical etching, often interpretive, yet infinitely more pleasing than their earlier efforts. This was to continue, encouraged by the rise of landscape painting in Britain and the work of Turner and Constable in the 19th century and the engravers who worked after them.

The Smith family appears to have originated in the Guildford area, where William the eldest of this painting trio was born in 1707. The brothers George and John (1717–64) often worked together and this small etched plate carries the names of both. The spirited etching of the trees, and the group of buildings and hayricks in the middle foreground is rather marred by the cross hatching of the sky and the somewhat heavy and laboured treatment of the water.

The reader interested in original etching should seek Shaw Sparrow's excellent *Book of British Etching from Barlow to Seymour Haden,* now much overdue for re-printing. Shaw Sparrow comments on the brothers as follows:- 'It was in 1770 that two Smiths of Chichester brought out in London, from John Boydell's shop, Cheapside, their collection of fifty-three prints, etchings and engravings, "after their own paintings and other Masters". Other Masters is a funny touch of unintended self praise, implying that the Smiths themselves are Masters, not humble pioneers born in a somnolent city where their father is a baker, and a cooper, and a Baptist minister. George Smith modelled his painting on Claude and Poussin, and once, by a sort of miracle, he defeated even Richard Wilson in open competition, winning a premium from the Society of Arts'.

Despite the earlier 'open' work of etchers like Hollar and Francis Place, British landscape etching in the 18th century appears to have suffered from being too closely allied to the linear approach of the line engraver until this technique was discarded by the work of John Sell Cotman, John Crome and others in the early 19th century.

Process: Etching   Source: Private, 1980

Size: $4\frac{3}{8}'' \times 5\frac{1}{2}''$ (111 × 140mm)

Watermark: None

No. 32　Original etching by Smith of Chichester *Author's Collection*

Paul Sandby R.A., c. 1725–1809

One of my favourite prints in the collection is this large fine aquatint view of Worcester, etched, aquatinted and published by Paul Sandby in 1778. The print bustles with interest and the commercial life of the river Severn that was used to ferry clay to the nearby porcelain works. In the background, quiet yet dominant, lies the beautiful Cathedral Church of Worcester, last resting place of that notorious English monarch King John.

The Sandby brothers, Paul and his elder brother (Thomas 1721–98) were natives of Nottingham and both were draughtsmen of ability, Thomas working for the Duke of Cumberland and Paul working in Scotland for the Board of Ordnance after the rebellion of 1745. Some of Paul's early drawings date from this period in Scotland. In 1745 the Duke of Cumberland was appointed Ranger of Windsor Great Park and took Thomas with him as his deputy, where he remained until his death at the Deputy Ranger's Lodge in 1798.

In 1751 Paul Sandby left the Board of Ordnance, joining his brother at Windsor, assisting him with his work in the park and the building of Virginia Water. Whilst there, Paul produced a great many delightful watercolours of Windsor, many of which are now in the Royal Collection there. From 1768 to 1796 he was drawing master at the Royal Military Academy at Woolwich and it was during this period that both this example and his famous aquatints of Wales were produced.

Both brothers were founder members of the Royal Academy and many art historians regard Paul as the father of the Early English Watercolour School. He is also regarded as being responsible for the introduction of aquatint engraving into Britain and his *Twelve Views in Wales*, published in 1776, was the first aquatint book of its kind to be published in Britain. This volume carries a dedication to the Honourable Charles Greville from whom Sandby obtained the secret of the aquatint process. His *Twelve Views In North Wales*, also published in 1776, is dedicated to the Honourable Sir Watkin Williams Wynn, Bart., a famous Welsh patron of the arts and godfather of the ill-fated William Wynne Ryland (J. R. Abbey—*Scenery of Great Britain & Ireland*, page 343).

Paul Sandby produced a great many smaller etchings and aquatints and some of his topographical drawings were reproduced in *The Itinerant*, published for J. Walker in 1799, which also contain prints after many of the artists of the Early English School, including J. M. W. Turner, Thomas Girtin, Edward Dayes and Francis Nicholson. These large aquatint plates executed by Paul Sandby are now rare and costly.

Process: Aquatint   Source: Private, 1972

Size: $12\frac{3}{4}'' \times 19\frac{7}{8}''$ (324 × 505mm)

Watermark: IHS and cross within oval (*c.*1750)

No. 33   Worcester by Paul Sandby R.A.—aquatint *Author's Collection*

Thomas Gainsborough R.A., 1727–1788

This famous painter was born at Sudbury, Suffolk in 1727 and was a pupil of Gravelot. Despite his importance as a painter, Gainsborough etched a number of plates, both in soft-ground etching and aquatint, some of which were later copied by Paul Sandby.

This print was acquired for the collection some years ago because I had not previously seen an original print example (as I then thought) by Thomas Gainsborough. *The Gipsies* appears to have been first published by J. Wood in March 1759, although Shaw Sparrow lists a later issue bearing Boydell's imprint in 1764, some five years later. Certainly, the style of the etching is very laboured and the detailed finishing suggests the training of a line engraver rather than that of an etcher. When compared with Gainsborough's soft-ground etchings of landscape, it is impossible to believe that he could have been responsible for more than the outline detail on this particular print.

The print had been badly damaged by damp and a considerable portion along the right-hand margin had disintegrated, although the wording 'Engraved and Finished by J. Wood' was clearly visible. I find it difficult to accept that Gainsborough was personally involved in any of the detail work on the item and think it more likely that Wood made a copy after an original painting by the master, which he (Gainsborough) had possibly reproduced as an etching. A reference in Slater to a John Wood (c. 1720–1780) lists him as an engraver and a pupil of Chatelain and credits him with '"Gipsies", after Gainsborough, proof, £1.5s' (1921).

Gainsborough was one of the original members of the Royal Academy when it was established by George III in 1768. He was later elected to the Council of the Academy but after a number of disputes he did not exhibit there after 1784. He had moved from Bath to London some time previously in order to compete with Sir Joshua Reynolds who, in addition to being knighted, had also become President of the Royal Academy.

Any readers who are already print collectors will have noticed a reference on certain prints where the figures are engraved by a particular engraver and the landscape detail by someone else. In other words, two engravers working on the same plate. This was quite common practice in painting where the pupils of a particular artist would be employed on the less important aspects of a picture. Gainsborough was never party to this procedure and always painted the entire work himself. He is well represented by his paintings in the principal galleries and museums of this country but his original prints are rare.

Process: Etchings/line engraving   Source: Private, 1978

Size: 18⅜″ × 16¼″ (467 × 413mm)

Watermark: None

108

No. 34 The Gipsies by Thomas Gainsborough RA—line engraving and etching *Author's Collection*

Samuel and Nathaniel Buck fl. 1721–59

The major output of topographical work in the early eighteenth century resulted from the labours of the brothers Samuel and Nathaniel Buck, who spent much of their working lives visiting, sketching, and engraving the towns, cities, castles, abbeys and churches of the country. Their important contribution to British topography was, however, the production of eighty-three large panoramic views of major towns and cities that were prepared by a mixture of line engraving and etching.

The *South prospect of Berwick upon Tweed* (illustrated) is typical of the charming if somewhat primitive approach the brothers brought to their work. Each view carries a key-plate listing the important buildings and this is supported by a finely executed copper plate historical note on the particular town or city. The plates were originally issued in black and white but careful and sympathetic hand colouring often results in prints of considerable beauty, value and interest.

The panoramic views were bound into books and so a centre fold will often be detected on examples found today. Some will be 'laid down' where the print has been stuck to a card backing. This backing will need to be removed before the print can be cleaned (see note on cleaning and restoration). Some of the original copper plates are still in existence so modern 're-strikes' are to be expected.

The brothers produced a series of smaller views—some four hundred and twenty in all and about one third of the size of the large panoramas. These also have several lines of descriptive text beneath the engraving and are mostly of castle and cathedral ruins that seem to have little appeal for today's collector. Notable exceptions include Ludlow Castle, Montacute Priory and Lacock Nunnery. This latter property was formerly the home of Fox-Talbot, the pioneer of photography, and is now a museum in the care of the National Trust.

There are some excellent full size reproductions of the large panoramic views issued by Messrs Traylen's, Booksellers of Guildford, who also publish two fine colour plate books on the Shotter Boys views of London.

Process: Line engraving/etching   Source: Auction, 1970

Size: $9\frac{3}{4}'' \times 31''$ (248 $\times$ 787mm)

Watermark: None

110

No. 35   South Prospect of Berwick on Tweed by S. & N. Buck—etching *Author's Collection*

Jean Baptiste Le Prince 1734–c.84

The French painter and etcher Jean Baptiste Le Prince is thought to have been the originator of the powdered resin ground method of aquatinting, a process he is said to have communicated to the Englishman the Hon. Charles Greville. Greville in turn is believed to have acquainted Paul Sandby with the process. Sandby later claimed that his application of the process was quite different and involved dissolving the resin particles in alcohol. Whatever the merits of the case, Sandby can certainly claim to be the first Englishman to produce a topographical plate book using the aquatint method.

The success of aquatint for illustration was established by the impetus provided by Sandby for the process and by the year 1792 a number of British publishers were producing books containing aquatint plates. The process also gained ground in France, where it was used for portraiture, a practice that was unknown in Britain.

When I first started collecting I purchased a bundle of prints in a saleroom and was surprised to find an aquatint signed by Le Prince amongst them. The item carries the title *Vue des Environs de Nerva* and is dated 1773. The print displays a considerable amount of line-etching that appears to have been executed after the aquatint ground was applied. This would be difficult unless drypoint work was carried out after the ground had been bitten.

According to F. L. Wilder, Le Prince appears to have been a musician as well as an artist-etcher. He travelled widely and even went to Russia where he was presented to the Czar. On one voyage the ship on which he was travelling was captured by British pirates whom he managed to entertain by playing his violin. He married a lady of wealth who was more than twice his age, made a great deal of money, all of which he spent, and died leaving a fine collection of creditors.

In Britain the aquatint process reached its zenith in the 1840's and then gave way to the cheaper and speedier processes of lithography. Many fine aquatint books were produced by publishers like Ackermann, Orme, Bowyer, Jenkins and others and a great many individual plates covering topography, field sports, ornithology and the like were published. Today examples of the process are scarce and expensive.

Process: Aquatint   Source: Private, 1968

Size: $7\frac{3}{4}'' \times 9\frac{3}{4}''$ (197 $\times$ 248mm)

Watermark: None

No. 36   Vue des Environs de Nerva by J. B. Le Prince—aquatint *Author's Collection*

Thomas Ryder 1746–1810

Thomas Ryder was one of the leading stipple engravers of the late 18th century and a typical example of his work is this decorative engraving of a *Visit to the Woman of the Lime Trees*, published by Watts in 1786. As mentioned earlier, the development of stipple engraving in Britain was largely due to the influence of Francesco Bartolozzi but much of the appeal of the process relied on the ability of the printers of the day to produce the prints in colours by applying these directly to the printing plate.

The popularity of stipple engravings printed in colours was greatly enhanced by the publication by Colnaghi in 1797 of thirteen plates after paintings by Francis Wheatley R.A. of *The Cries of London*, engraved by the leading stipple engravers of the period, namely Shiavonetti, Vendramini, Cardon and Gaugain. Early issues were printed in colours and the high prices realised by some of the sets on their return to the salerooms produced a mystique that survives to the present time. The series was also produced in mezzotint by Thomas Appleton in the early twentieth century. Since that time a succession of reproductions and deliberate forgeries have gone some way to meet the demand from that section of the art buying public that lies outside the skill and expertise of the professional print dealer. There are, no doubt, a great many homes in the kingdom whose owners are sure that they possess a genuine set of Wheatley's *Cries* but there is perhaps little likelihood of their reading any book likely to contribute to their knowledge on the subject! The possibility of today's collector finding one of the original Wheatley *Cries of London* is fairly remote but there are numerous examples by other stipple engravers of that period that are worth collecting, regardless of whether they were printed in colours or not.

The important painter and mezzotint engraver J. R. Smith was attracted to the process, as was William Ward, Samuel Cousins, Caroline Watson, Charles Knight, William Nutter, William Dickinson and, of course, the master himself, Francesco Bartolozzi. A great many 19th century re-prints were printed in red or brown ink and subsequently hand coloured and these items are worth only a fraction of the price of the early impressions printed in colours. The newcomer to print collecting would be unwise to trust their own judgement if attempting to purchase prints of this kind and the services of a reputable professional dealer should be sought.

Process: Stipple engraving   Source: The late Lord Methuen R.A.

Size: 8″ by 6¼″ oval (203 × 159mm)

Watermark: None

No. 37   Visit to a Woman of the Lime Trees by Thomas Ryder—stipple
engraving *Author's Collection*

James Gillray 1756–1815

This important Georgian caricaturist was a Lancastrian by birth and possibly a student of William Wynne Ryland, who was hanged for forgery in 1783. Gillray is known to have spent some time in the Royal Academy Schools before commencing his career as the most vitriolic caricaturist this country has ever produced. Most of his work was published by Miss Hannah Humphrey, who looked after him when insanity overtook him in 1810. His prints depict most aspects of life in Georgian and Regency Britain and include fashion, politics and the Royal family; in particular King George III and the Prince Regent. It is doubtful whether any of today's cartoonists would pursue the extremes of bad taste sometimes practiced by Gillray without the risk of being prosecuted for defamation.

This political example, which he captioned *The Feast of Reason and the flow of Soul—i.e. The Wits of the Age, setting the Table in a Roar* is one of the more innocuous in the collection and depicts certain of the Opposition wits ridiculed as favoured companions of George Hanger, who is seated at the lower end of the table with a cudgel in his boot. Courtnay chairs the proceedings partnered by Fox, Sheridan and M. A. Taylor (British Museum No. 8984). Although Gillray appears to have attacked all the political leaders of his day, regardless of party, the Tories gave him a pension!

His prints brought about a collecting vogue in their own day, often with customers waiting at Humphrey's shop whilst the bright and sometimes careless hand-washes were applied by a small team of colourists. The 'gay-blades', and the not so gay, visited one another's homes and clubs, taking along their most recent and outrageous acquisitions, a practice that continued well into Victorian times. After Gillray's death many of the plates were re-issued by Thomas McLean in two volumes, *The Genuine Works of James Gillray* containing upwards of five hundred plates printed on both sides of the leaves. They were re-printed again by Bohn in the mid-nineteenth century when numbers were added to the plates.

Gillray's work is now keenly sought by collectors and some originals have been known to command high prices. Needless to say, lithographic copies are not uncommon and the intending collector might do better to seek the work of the less popular artists, including the Heath family, Henry (fl. 1830), William (fl. 1820). Some of George Cruikshank's (1792–1878) work can still be found quite cheaply, as can that of the Dighton's. The humorous angling plate on the cover of this book was bought some years ago for the princely sum of one pound and as any pike fisherman will know, the print is far from being a flight of fancy!

Process: Etching   Source: Private, 1976

Size: 9″ by 13½″ (229 × 343mm)

Watermark: None

No. 38 'The Feast of Reason & the Flow of Soul' by James Gillray—etching *Author's Collection*

Joseph Constantine Stadler fl. 1782–1814

The rivers of Britain have provided inspiration for generations of artists and engravers, not least the river Thames, depicted here with this double-page aquatint of *London from Lambeth*, published in 1796 by J and J. Boydell. The print appeared in the now famous two volume work—*History of the River Thames*, a rare and expensive topographical book prepared from drawings made by Joseph Farington, R.A. (1747–1821) a highly respected Royal Academician and former pupil of Richard Wilson. The seventy-six plates were aquatinted by J. C. Stadler, one of the leading engravers of the late 18th century and himself a publisher of a series of plates on the Brighton 'Pavillon'.

Seventy-four of the plates are single page and two, *London from Lambeth* and *London from Greenwich*, are double page. These larger plates are in great demand and usually command high prices, so perhaps the modest collector interested in river scenery should look for certain of the smaller and earlier aquatint plates that can still be bought for a ten-pound note. Artist Samuel Ireland published his *Picturesque Views on the River Thames* in 1792 containing fifty-two delightfully primitive topographical views of the river from its source to the sea. The following year he issued a work of similar title on the river Medway with twenty-eight plates. Two further books deal with the rivers Wye and the Warwickshire Avon (31 plates). His *Picturesque Views of the Severn* was published in lithography by Charles Hullmandel in 1824, although by this time Ireland was dead.

William Westall ARA was well known for his topographical work in the 19th century and a great many steel engravings were prepared after his drawings. He personally lithographed some thirty-five views of Thames scenery in 1824 and selected plates from this larger work are sometimes found with plates of Richmond, Eton, Windsor and Oxford as *Twenty Five Views on The Thames*. Both Westall and Samuel Owen later worked on an Ackermann production *Picturesque Tour of the River Thames* that contained some twenty-six aquatint plates issued in 1828.

Mention has already been made of Cooke's *Thames Scenery* and a plate from this appears elsewhere in the book. This was to be one of the last copper plate topographical books of the early nineteenth century and by the time William Tombleson issued his well known *Thames and Medway* in the early 1830's, the era of the copper plate book had virtually ended. The seventy-nine plates in Tombleson's book were etched on steel in the manner of line engravings and the less popular areas can still be bought fairly cheaply. However, the London bridges and views of Windsor and Oxford and the river near London, tend to be more expensive.

Process: Aquatint

Source: John Orde, 1982

Size: $12\frac{1}{8}' \times 20\frac{5}{8}''$ (308 × 534mm)

Watermark: Whatman 1794

118

J Farington R.A. del.
Pub. June 1, 1795, by J. & J. Boydell, Shakspeare -
View of LONDON from Lambeth
- Gallery, Pall-Mall, and N.90, Cheapside.
J.C. Stadler sculp.

No. 39 London from Lambeth by J. C. Standler—aquatint *Author's Collection*

John Raphael Smith 1752–1812

This skilled and talented artist and engraver was born at Derby in 1752 the son of 'Smith of Derby', the landscape painter. Like his father, John's painting and engraving skills were entirely self taught and he commenced his artistic career by painting miniatures and then decided to attempt mezzotint engraving. He subsequently engraved many hundreds of mezzotint and stipple plates after the leading artists of the day, including Gainsborough, Reynolds, Romney and Morland. His versatility extended to work in both oil and crayon, as well as the running of a highly successful print shop.

This fine large mezzotint of The Prince of Wales is a very recent addition to the collection and carried a price-tag of eighteen pounds when purchased early in 1983. It has unfortunately been trimmed close to the edges of the engraved border, with resulting loss of plate-mark and is 'laid down'.

The print is framed and glazed in old glass whose 'rippled' quality is much more suited to old prints than is its modern counterpart. When framing items for the collection I use old glass whenever possible, although this tends to be brittle and is difficult to cut. Many of Smith's early works carry the wording 'engraved by J. R. Smith' but this example is probably a re-issue of an earlier plate with the imprint changed to 'Painted and engraved by J. R. Smith Mezzotinto Engraver to His Royal Highness the Prince of Wales'. Despite this honour and his distinguished career as a painter and engraver, Smith was never elected to membership of the Royal Academy.

Smith was a great personal friend of painter George Morland and both shared a keen interest in field sports and the tavern life of the time, so it is perhaps not surprising that he engraved a good many of Morland's pictures. The American War of Independence in 1776, and an ongoing state of war with France, doubtless contributed to the depression in Britain that seriously affected the print trade and caused Smith to close his shop and take to the road as a travelling artist. Matters were made worse because a great deal of the paper used by the British print trade had to be imported from the Continent, although it was at about this time that James Whatman opened his famous Turkey Paper Mill at Maidstone, and thereafter most of the fine prints of the 18th and 19th centuries were printed on his paper.

The contribution made by John Raphael Smith to British art in general, and print making in particular, has probably never been equalled by any other engraver. His prints are still in great demand and examples printed in colours command high prices. He was undertaking a commission in Doncaster in 1811 when he was suddenly taken ill and died shortly afterwards in his sixtieth year. He was buried in the local churchyard at Doncaster.

Process: Mezzotint   Source: Ian Brook Gallery, Wilton, 1983

Size: 17½″ by 23½″ (444 × 597mm)   Watermark: Laid down—non visible

No. 40   His Royal Highness George Prince of Wales by J. R. Smith—mezzotint
Author's Collection

Thomas Rowlandson 1756–1827

It is perhaps a little unfair to expect a traditional Victorian-like Samuel Redgrave in his *Dictionary of Artists of the English School* (1874) to see the art of Thomas Rowlandson as other than the work of a man 'who was careless and idle ... known in most of the London gaming houses'. Certainly, Rowlandson shared Morland's love of low life and this is reflected in much of his best work. Redgrave considered that Rowland's book illustrations for 'Dr Syntax' and 'The Dance of Death' were the two works by which he would be remembered.

Rowlandson's first important achievement was his *Loyal Volunteers of London and Environs* published by Ackermann in 1799. This magnificent book details some seventy-eight infantry and nine cavalry units which, according to Ackermann, were intended as much to combat the possibility of insurrection at home as they were to meet any threat from 'the crooked policy of our enemies abroad'. The entire work was etched by Rowlandson himself and the plates were subsequently aquatinted and hand coloured for the two hundred subscribers who had contributed to the publication. Ten years later Rowlandson and Pugin began to prepare the drawing for *The Microcosm of London*, which resulted in one hundred and four plates being etched and aquatinted, depicting the busy life of the City and its Institutions in the early nineteenth century. In this enterprise the unmistakable style of Rowlandson is clearly apparent in the groups of figures, whilst Pugin prepared the architectural backgrounds to the series.

Certainly Rowlandson indulged in a great amount of 'hack-work' for the book trade and many of his original watercolours prepared for the Prince Regent (now in the Royal Collection) display basic aspects of human nature in a way that give offence to many people even in these enlightened times. By contrast the collection of his watercolour drawings brought together by Albert H. Wiggin and now in the Boston Public Library (USA) enabled this far-sighted American to provide his fellow countrymen with a mirror of life in 18th century Britain prepared by this remarkably gifted artist and caricaturist.

It is interesting to compare the earlier work of William Hogarth, the moralist, with that of Rowlandson, for Rowlandson was no searcher after morality, merely depicting the everyday incidents of life as he saw them and leaving the judgements to others. This print of *The Glutton* was an early acquisition to the collection and it is typical of Rowlandson's style. The young of either sex are always beautiful, the middle aged or elderly are depicted with all the maladies of figure and form yet, surprisingly, are usually drawn with far greater vigour and character.

Process: Etching   Source: Private, 1974

Size: $9\frac{1}{4}'' \times 13\frac{1}{4}''$ (235 × 337mm)

Watermark: None

122

No. 41 'The Glutton' by Thomas Rowlandson—etching *Author's Collection*

George Morland 1763–1804

To many people George Morland represents all that is best in English rural painting. Many of his subjects display a freshness and simplicity that is as popular today as it was two hundred years ago. Did Morland know William Henry Pyne, I wonder? Both men shared an obvious love of the countryside and country-folk that George Baxter also captured with his famous series of oval prints nearly a century later (Plate 26).

Prints after Morland's paintings are legion, many executed by important engravers of the period, including his brother-in-law William Ward, J. R. Smith, Rowlandson, Vivares, S. W. Reynolds, S. Alken, and J. Fittler. His popularity and importance as a painter was, of course, greatly enhanced by the work of the print makers.

Herbert Baily lists well over two hundred engraved examples of his paintings in his book *George Morland* (see Bibliography), together with the sizes of the prints and the names of the various engravers. The *Country Butcher* illustrated is, unfortunately, one of the many fraudulent prints of his work issued early this century. It was originally fitted in an ornamental gilt frame, the glass of the picture having been painted black and a gold-leaf border added. Hardly the kind of expensive presentation one expects for a copy, which is precisely what the seller wanted the intending buyer to think!

Two engravings after this subject are known, one by W. Barnard measuring $18\frac{1}{8}'' \times 24\frac{1}{4}''$. The other by T. Gosse measures $17\frac{1}{2}'' \times 22''$. Our fake measures $16'' \times 20''$ and proves the importance of the tape-measure to the print collector.

Morland later married Ann Ward, sister of William Ward, the engraver and William married George's sister Maria. Sadly, Morland's drinking bouts and his unfortunate choice of associates led to constant quarrels that ended with the two men fighting a duel with pistols in a sandpit near their home. Fortunately neither managed to hit the other, whereupon the Morlands moved out, setting up home in Camden Town.

Morland's drinking and other excesses finally landed him heavily in debt and towards the end of his life he was in continual fear of being imprisoned for debt. After several strokes he died on the 29th October 1804 at the early age of forty-two.

Process: Hand coloured reproduction   Source: Private, 1970

Size: $16'' \times 20''$ (407 × 508mm)

Watermark: None

124

No. 42   The Country Butcher after George Morland—photo-mechanical *Author's Collection*

Samuel Drummond A.R.A. 1763–1844

One of the delights of print collecting is the opportunity the study provides to extend ones knowledge of the painters of a particular period as well as the personalities portrayed by their work. This portrait was originally painted by Samuel Drummond A.R.A., an historical painter of some stature, for he exhibited at the Royal Academy on no less than three hundred and three different occasions. Redgrave tells us that Drummond was born in London on the 25th December, 1763 and that his father fought with the Pretender in 1745 and was forced to flee the country. Young Samuel ran away to sea when he was only fourteen and stayed away some years. On his return he began to develop his interest in art and painting, despite a total lack of formal training. He first exhibited at the Royal Academy in 1791 and one of his important portraits is that of Sir Isambard Brunel.

Drummond figures prominently in the records of the British Institution and between the years 1807 and 1844 he exhibited some eighty four paintings, a great many of which were based on biblical subjects. His historic painting of Admiral de Winter surrendering his sword to Lord Duncan after the Battle of Camperdown was presented by the British Institution to the Royal Hospital at Greenwich.

This stipple portrait of Mr. James Asperne, a Cornhill Bookseller, is a small work of considerable merit, although little is known of the engraver concerned as his name does not appear in any of the standard reference books. The features of the sitter are particularly good and although there is some evidence of etching on the cravat and apron, and in the right background, the bulk of the portrait has been executed in pure stipple. The paintings and portrait prints of this period provide an invaluable record of the personalities of the time prior to the introduction of photography.

Mr. Asperne appears to have been a freemason of some importance and the caption beneath the print lists his various offices. As the print does not carry a publisher's imprint it is possibly from a book of the period devoted to freemasonry. Similar examples are keenly sought by collectors and are uncommon.

Process: Stipple engraving   Source: Tolley Gallery, 1974

Size: $9\frac{3}{8}'' \times 7\frac{3}{4}''$ (239 × 197mm)

Watermark: None

126

Painted by S. Drummond A.R.A.

Engraved by T. Blood.

Mr James Asperne

BOOKSELLER, CORNHILL,

Past Master of the FOUNDATION LODGE No. 96. And St Peter's No. 249

P.S.D. of the LODGE of Antiquity No. 1. And Grand Steward for 1814

No. 43   Mr James Asperne after Samuel Drummond A.R.A.—stipple
engraving *Author's Collection*

William Henry Pyne 1769–1843

W. H. Pyne was born in Holborn, London in 1769, the son of a leather merchant and entirely self-taught as far as his artistic talents were concerned. I bought his book of *Rustic Figures for the Embelishment of Landscape* (1814) from a venerable bookseller in Cecil Court, London, at least twenty years ago. My affection for his work shows no signs of abating as the years go by.

His earlier *Microcosm of Great Britain* published in 1803 did for the countryside what Rowlandson and Pugin attempted to do for London. The plate illustrated is typical of the whole for, unlike *the Microcosm of London*, Pyne does not need the familiarity of a particular building or institution to be in demand. Look at the wheel widths on the waggons that were designed to flatten the ruts in many of the unmade roads of the period but which, due to the increased weight of the waggons, only made them worse! Here are plates every farmer in the kingdom would love, were he to know them.

The plates are a mixture of etching and aquatint, well able to survive on their tonal quality without the aid of watercolour. Something more than a casual glance is necessary to appreciate them, not least a knowledge of the countryside and its tools and tasks. There is one plate in the series to delight all anglers; proving then as now the old adage—a fool on one end and a worm on the other—with even bigger fools watching!

Two other important works produced by Pyne were his *Costume of Great Britain* (1805) and *Royal Residences* (1819). The latter aquatints are sometimes sometimes found printed in colour although the plates are somewhat on the small size. This venture ended in financial disaster.

Pyne was an author of some merit, writing several books under the pen name of Ephraim Hardcastle. He was a founder member of the Old Watercolour Society and an exhibitor at the Royal Academy on a number of occasions.

Process: Etching and Aquatint   Source: Eiddon Morgan, 1980

Size: $8\frac{3}{4}'' \times 11\frac{3}{8}''$ (222 × 289mm)

Watermark: None

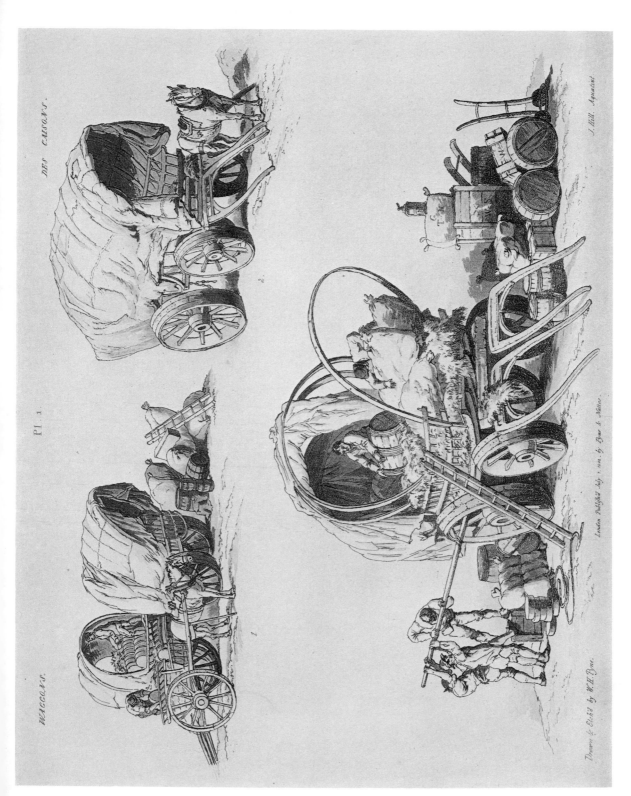

No. 44   Study of Waggons by W. H. Pyne—etching & aquatint *Author's Collection*

William Daniell R.A. 1769–1837

The monumental work in aquatint as far as British topography is concerned is William Daniell's *A Voyage Round Great Britain*, published in parts and volume form between 1814 and 1825 and comprising no less than three hundred and eight plates, mostly in pure aquatint.

Over a period of eleven years Daniell's engraving output must have been prodigious averaging two aquatint plates per month, which for a work in aquatint appears incredible, if not impossible. All the plates display a remarkable consistency of quality, matched only by the soft and careful hand colouring.

The tour started at Portreath, Cornwall, and progressed along the north Devon coast to Wales, along the west coast of England and Scotland and then back down the eastern coastline and the south coast (including the Isle of Wight) to finish at Land's End.

The plates have a fine grain not usually found on aquatints of this early period but William was brought up in a hard school. He accompanied his uncle Thomas Daniell R.A. to India at the age of fourteen and some ten years were to pass before they returned to England to prepare *Oriental Scenery*, possibly the most beautiful colour plate book ever published.

There is also a large and rare series of London views in aquatint, prepared some years before he embarked upon the Great Britain voyage. These include Greenwich Park, The Tower and Pool of London, London Bridge, St. Pauls, Somerset House, and Westminster Abbey and Bridge.

The view of Amlwch Harbour is one of a number of similar prints in the collection chosen for their shipping interest. The extent of their aquatint quality cannot really be appreciated from a book illustration. The reader may be assured that the mast and most of the rigging on the vessel entering harbour is not the result of etched line-work but is executed in pure aquatint.

The printing plates are still in existence and were issued as a limited edition some years ago. Original examples carry Whatman dated watermarks. There is evidence of the fine ruled line-work breaking down on the borders of some later re-prints.

Process: Pure aquatint   Source: Tolley Gallery, 1969

Size: $6\frac{1}{2}'' \times 9\frac{3}{8}''$ (165 × 239mm)

Watermark: Whatman 1813

No. 45   A View of Amlwch Harbour by William Daniell R.A.—aquatint *Author's Collection*

Thomas Girtin 1775–1802

Two great English artists were born within weeks of one another in the year 1755. Thomas Girtin was to prove himself an outstanding watercolourist and etcher before his untimely death in 1802 at the early age of twenty-seven. His great friend and boon companion during those early years as struggling artists, was J. M. W. Turner. As youngsters both worked for John Raphael Smith, their leisure time being spent colouring prints for sale in his shop. They doubtless met George Morland who was a great friend of Smith's and, perhaps, the older and kindly Paul Sandby put in a word, so that their first published work appeared along side his in *The Itinerent*. Some time previously young Girtin had been thrown into prison having complained to Dayes the architect (to whom he was articled) that he was not learning the profession by simply applying washes to architectural drawings.

There are some delightful insights into Girtin's early work in Walter Thornbury's fascinating book on *The Life of J. M. W. Turner RA*. In his twenty fifth year Turner was elected to membership of the Royal Academy, thereafter signing his work J. M. W. Turner, rather than the abbreviated W. Turner that he had used previously. For Girtin, concentrating on watercolour, the Academy doors were closed. In 1801, however, he sent his first oil to the Academy, a painting of 'Bolton Bridge' and in the spring of the following year he visited France, hoping that a change of climate would improve his failing health.

The print illustrated forms part of a set of twenty drawings Girtin made whilst at Paris during the shaky Peace of Amiens. Having been forbidden to sketch by the suspicious French he made the drawings whilst being driven round the city and its outskirts in a horse and carriage! Returning to England in May 1802 he commenced work by soft-ground etching the twenty plates. By the end of June he had completed ten plates, a further four followed in July, in August three more, September two, and the final one on the 4th October. A month later Girtin was dead.

After his death, his brother John took over the publication of the plates and the aquatint was applied to them by F. C. Lewis. A tragic fire at Girtin's premises some years later destroyed many of his brother's best works and his wife, who was ill at the time, died in his arms as he carried her from the flaming building. Thornbury quotes a written comment made by Turner about his great f·iend whose loss he felt so deeply—'Had Tom Girtin lived, I should have ɔtarved'—an obvious tribute to Girtin's great ability as an artist and etcher.

Process: Soft-ground etching
          and aquatint

Source: Moreshead Collection, 1970

Size: 5″ × 18¾″ (128 × 477mm)

Watermark: None

No. 46   View of the Village of *Chaillot* by Thomas Girtin—soft ground etching & aquatint *Author's Collection*

J. M. W. Turner R.A., P.P.—1775–1851

Joseph Mallord William Turner was born on the 23rd April 1775 in the parish of St. Paul, Covent Garden where his name may still be seen in the Register of Baptisms for the 14th May, 1775. His father was a hairdresser and the family lived on the west end of Maiden Lane as one approaches from Southampton Street. Turner's youthful friendship with Thomas Girtin and their work together colouring in the print shop of J. R. Smith has already been noted. His first published work appeared in Walker's *Itinerant* copper plate magazine dated 1st May, 1794, and was followed by a view of Chepstow issued on the 1st November, 1794. In these early plates the captions read 'from an original drawing by W. Turner' and Walter Thornbury states that Turner did not add his full initials to his work until he was elected R.A. in 1802. Over the years I have managed to collect most of the early prints from Walker's publications by both Turner and Girtin at a cost of pence rather than pounds.

Turner was a keen fisherman and the reader will not be surprised to learn that many of his paintings and the prints produced from his drawings reflect his angling instincts, as for example his view of Carlisle published by Walker in 1797. He was an astute businessman and according to Thornbury derived the greater part of his income from royalties received from the loan of his drawings for reproduction purposes. When Charles Turner the mezzotint engraver agreed to produce the plates for the *Liber Studiorum* he repeatedly returned to Turner as the plates were completed asking for a review of the prices, explaining that for the amount of work involved he could not complete them for the sum originally agreed. Turner flatly refused to compromise over the price— a bargain was a bargain. After completing the nineteenth plate in the series, Charles Turner refused to undertake any further work on the project, vowing he would never work for Turner again and his business association with the great man ended.

The example illustrated, the town of Basle, was the fourth or fifth plate mezzotinted by Charles Turner, published in 1807. The project met with mixed success and Turner finally abandoned the publication of the remaining twenty plates in 1819. Needless to say, this is one of the few print issues of Turner's work where the great man actually undertook some of the etching on the plates. These Liber plates are now rare and expensive.

Turner died in Chelsea on the 18th December, 1851, having bequeathed many of his finest paintings to the nation with a request that they should form a Turner Gallery for the benefit of future generations. This request is still under active consideration some one hundred and thirty years later!

Process: Etching and mezzotint   Source: Private, 1976

Size: $7\frac{1}{4}''\times10\frac{1}{4}''$ (184 × 260mm)   Watermark: None

No. 47   Basle by J. M. W. Turner R.A.—*mezzotint Author's Collection*

William Bernard 1778–1855 and George Cooke 1781–1834

The rise of the topographical print in Britain was largely due to the introduction of the illustrated copper plate books of the late 18th century. These enabled the drawings of the artists of the early English Watercolour School to be brought before the public and did much to popularise the work of Paul Sandby, Thomas Girtin, J. M. W. Turner, John Varley, David Cox and other artists of that period.

As the demand for illustrated books increased there was a marked improvement in the engraved quality of the work. It is interesting to compare illustrations from the *Copper Plate Magazine* with those of Britton and the Cookes', published some fifteen to twenty years later. Both brothers trained as line engravers, the younger George being the father of Edward William Cooke, later to distinguish himself as a marine painter.

This copper etching of Lechlade is one of seventy-five prints from their *Thames Scenery*, published in 1818, and may well have provided William Tombleson with his inspiration for a similar work on steel some years later when the Medway towns were added. By this time a great many of the book illustrations being produced by engravers were the result of etching, rather than line engraving; the speedier process provided by etching the plates being necessary to meet a greatly increased demand.

The Cooke brothers were some of the first engravers to work after the paintings and drawings of J. M. W. Turner and their *Picturesque Views on the Southern Coast of England* was first issued in parts from 1814 and as a complete work in 1826. Decorative copper plates from the books of this period are bound to be scarcer than their later steel counterparts. One of the finest copper plate works is Wiltshire born John Britton's *Picturesque Antiquities of English Cities*, with sixty plates in which the views of Lincoln and Salisbury are particularly fine. The title is important when looking for prints from this work. There are other Britton titles that are similar but which contain ruined architecture that is of little interest to today's collector.

Process: Copper line-etching   Source: Tolley Gallery, 1978

Size: $4\frac{1}{2}'' \times 7\frac{3}{4}''$ (114 × 197mm)

Watermark: None

No. 48   Lechlade by G. Cooke—line etching *Author's Collection*

Lowes Dickinson 1819–1908

Some years ago I was attempting a little research on Lowes Dickinson, an artist and lithographer who worked for Charles Hullmandel. In a copy of W. L. Wilder's *Print Prices Current 1926/7* I found a reference to Dickinson having lithographed a portrait of *John Booth, Huntsman with Hounds* after a painting by John Ferneley. I searched for my namesake for many years without success until a visit to Yorkshire took me to Harrogate. There in the Barnard Gallery, looking down from an elegant Bird's-eye maple frame astride a white hunter, sat the red-coated figure of John Booth. There was a look of astonishment on the young lady assistant's face when she read the signature on the cheque. 'You wouldn't have got him for that price if I had known what they called you' she said with a mischievous smile.

Lowes Dickinson, who lithographed the print, was born in London in 1819 and enjoyed an enviable reputation as a portrait painter and sporting artist. His subjects included many famous and important people, including Queen Victoria, Charles Kingsley, General Gordon and Gladstone. He was keenly interested in social reform and founded the Working Men's College, where he taught drawing and painting in association with John Ruskin and Gabriel Rossetti. Dickinson was a regular contributor to the Royal Academy, where he exhibited on some one hundred and nine occasions.

The painter, John Ferneley was born in the Quorn Country at Thrussington in 1781, or thereabouts, and is possibly one of the least known of our important animal painters. He was a pupil of Ben Marshall along with Abraham Cooper. Marshall, it seems, decided to return to Newmarket after some twenty years as a highly sought-after animal painter in London. Cooper apparently wondered at the wisdom of the move whereupon Marshall said 'Stop, stop, though! I have good reason for going. I discover many a man who will pay me fifty guineas for painting his horse who thinks ten guineas too much to pay for painting his wife!' (Shaw Sparrow—*British Sporting Artists*).

Many of Ferneley's animal portraits were painted for the hunting aristocracy and nobility of the day. His work did not appear to attract the attention of the print makers, nor is it likely that many of his wealthy patrons would have wished it to do so. His friend and supporter, Francis Grant, (later Sir Francis Grant, President of the Royal Academy) by painting Meets of various hunts discovered there was a lively demand for the prints after his paintings, and prints after his work are very popular. John Ferneley exhibited at the Royal Academy on some twenty-two occasions and at the British Institution and the Suffolk Street Gallery. He died on 3rd June, 1860 and was buried at his birthplace, in the churchyard at Thrussington.

Process: Lithograph   Source: Barnard Gallery, 1971

Size: $17\frac{1}{2}'' \times 2\frac{1}{2}''$ (445 × 572mm)   Watermark: None

138

No. 49   John Booth by Lowes Dickinson—lithograph *Author's Collection*

Samuel Prout 1783–1853

This Devonshire artist was born at Plymouth in 1783 and educated at the local Grammar School. During his early period he worked for John Britton in London, returning home in 1805 mainly due to ill health and thereafter painting local scenery. He became a drawing master and a number of his works were published by Ackermann with teaching studies in mind.

Prout visited the continent after the end of the war with France and a great many of his watercolours depict the architecture of the cathedrals and churches of northern France. The example of his work illustrated was published in aquatint by Robert Bowyer in 1825 and was one of four by him included in Bowyer's *Selection of Fac-similes of Water Colour Drawings from the Works of the most distinguished British Artists*. This work contains twelve plates and, in the first state, the prints are without titles. It was re-issued in 1828 with six additional plates.

Prints from the Bowyer stable are invariably aquatints of high quality. There are some fine topographical plates of European cities, including Berlin, Leipsic, Dantzic, Amsterdam, Dresden and Hamburgh (the spelling is taken from the prints!). There is also a very fine double-page aquatint of the Kremlin. All these prints are from illustrated books to do with the Napoleonic campaigns in Europe and Russia.

Prout's architectural studies were greatly admired during the Victorian era and many of his students painted in his style. His nephew John Skinner Prout (1806–1876), shared his uncle's interest in old architecture and lithography. He lived for some time in Bristol and published a book illustrating the antiquities of the city. He personally lithographed *The Castles and Abbeys of Monmouthshire*, issued in 1838. These are fairly large plates employing a single tint-stone but appear to attract little interest outside the county. Collectors interested in Australia or Tasmania prints may be surprised to find Skinner Prout's work reproduced in Booth's *Australia* (which he visited as a young man), although the work was not published until shortly before his death in 1876.

Process: Aquatint   Source: Tolley Gallery, 1970

Size: $13\frac{1}{8}''$ × $10\frac{1}{8}''$ (333 × 257mm)

Watermark: None

No. 50   Fountain of the Stone Cross, Rouen after Samuel Prout—aquatint
Author's Collection

Henry Alken 1784–1851

No other British sporting artist ever brought humour to the hunting field with anything like the skill of Henry Alken. His parents had fled Denmark in the early 1770's due to the national unrest in the country and were living in London at the time of his birth in 1784. Very little is known of his early career but it seems probable that Samuel Alken the sporting painter was his uncle and may have been responsible for encouraging his early efforts as an artist and etcher.

Alken's first hunting prints were published in 1813 under his own name but thereafter he used the pseudonym 'Ben Tally Ho' until about 1820, when prints bearing his name began to appear with great regularity. His most important work was *The National Sports of Great Britain*, published by McLean in 1821, and containing fifty aquatints printed in colour prepared by J. Clark. He and Sutherland aquatinted many of Alken's subsequent prints.

Alken is perhaps best remembered for his *Night Riders of Nacton*, or *The First Steeple Chase on Record*; a set of four aquatints providing a graphic account of a race between officers from the Cavalry Barracks at Ipswich with the riders attired in nightshirts. The set was first published by Rudolph Ackermann in 1839 but sales appear to have been disappointing and the plates were sold to publisher Ben Brooks. Prints from the original Ackermann issue are rare and examples with a forged publisher's imprint are not unknown. The printing plates are still in use today and modern impressions still carry the imprint of Ben Brooks. A great many reprints of Alken's work appeared in the late 19th century, often without publisher's imprint. The majority of his prints were issued either by Thomas McLean, S. & J. Fuller or Rudolph Ackermann.

Many nineteenth century sporting prints were varnished and hung without glass in the manner of oil paintings. These are usually found today badly yellowed and darkened by age. Despite the usual canvas backing to the print, this treatment has caused the paper to crack and distort and presents a near impossible task for the restorer. The print illustrated had been treated in this way and an otherwise fine impression has lost much of its former glory.

Process: Etching/aquatint   Source: Private, 1983

Size: $8\frac{3}{8}''$ × $12\frac{3}{4}''$ (213 × 324mm)

Watermark: None

142

TURNING THE MAN BONEY COULDN'T TURN!
or

The Duke.—*Open the gate my man! Open the gate.* Bunchclod. *Ni'! Ni'! Measter says no one's to pass through here.*

2nd Horseman.—*BUT ITS THE DUKE!* Bunchclod. *Ar doesn't care, Measter says no' one's to pass through.*

The Duke.—*(Giving him a Sovereign) That's right my man always obey orders.*

Bunchclod. *(Eyeing the Duke as he turned away) E'DODS! OIVE TURNED THE MAN BONEY COULDN'T TURN!*

London, Published July 20th 1843, by R.Ackermann, at his Eclipse Sporting Gallery, 191,Regent Street.

No. 51 'Turning the Man Boney Couldn't Turn' after Henry Alken—aquatint *Author's Collection*

Thomas Miles Richardson 1784–1848

This important north country artist and lithographer was born at Newcastle upon Tyne on the 15th May, 1784, where his father was headmaster of the local Grammar School. He was apprenticed to an engraver in the city but on the death of his father succeeded him as head of St. Andrew's Grammar School. He commenced sketching and painting as a hobby. Seven years later he resigned from teaching and commenced a new career as a professional artist.

He worked in oils and watercolours and painted many landscapes in the vicinity of his native Newcastle, including a view of Newcastle from Gateshead Fell which was bought by the City. He exhibited at the Royal Academy on a number of occasions and was a regular contributor to the New Watercolour Society. His published work includes a set of seven lithographs of Shotley Bridge Spa, prepared by himself and his son Thomas Miles Richardson (Jnr), who also contributed one drawing to *Scotland Delineated*. (See J. D. Harding.)

This view of Grey Street, Newcastle, was published by F. Loraine whose print shop appears in the right foreground. Two tint-stones appear to have been used with subsequent hand colouring to the figures and shop facias. Mr. Loraine has the rare distinction of being the only trader whose name is correctly delineated on his signboard. In the case of the Queen's Head and G. Franks, the 's' appears in reverse.

It is interesting to compare the coaches; the rugged and somewhat basic local 'commuter' outside the Queen's Head is in marked contrast to the well sprung and up-dated model with its liveried driver and footman a little further along the street. The print is not unlike the series of London street scenes lithographed by Thomas Shotter Boys in the early eighteen-forties and was probably issued at about the same time. The artist has inserted his initials on the pavement, a practice frequently adopted by both Boys and J. D. Harding.

A number of provincial publishers issued work of this kind in the 19th century, although printing often took place in London. The railway view at Bath Ford, Bath, is a similar example. At that time these prints were purely for local interest and it is unlikely that a particular issue exceeded more than two hundred copies. Comparable examples today are likely to be rare and costly.

Process: Lithograph—
        two tint-stones

Source: Bath Antique Market, 1980

Size: 11″ × 16¼″ (271 × 413mm)

Watermark: None

No. 52 Grey Street, Newcastle by T. M. Richardson—lithograph *Author's Collection*

Thomas Sutherland c. 1785–1850

One of the most important aquatint engravers at work during the Regency period was Thomas Sutherland and prints carrying his name are usually of outstanding quality. Little appears to be known of his early life but some of his prints date from the Waterloo period. He engraved a great many sporting subjects, working after Alken, Herring, R. B. Davis and other notables. Many of his maritime plates are after Huggins, Heath or Whitcombe. In 1814 James Jenkins issued *The Martial Achievements of Great Britain and Her Allies from 1799 to 1815,* a fine aquatint work containing some fifty-two plates that were mostly aquatinted by Sutherland. A sister volume, *The Naval Achievements of Great Britain, From the Year 1793 to 1817*, was published by Jenkins in 1817 and, again, Sutherland prepared most of the fifty-five plates that were mainly after oil paintings by Thomas Whitcombe.

My copy of *Naval Achievements* is watermarked 1821 and it is likely that, apart from a re-issue of the book at about that date, some prints may have been pulled and issued from individual plates. In 1922 a copy of *Naval Achievements* was sold by Messrs Sotheby for twenty-four pounds (Print Prices Current), whereas today a copy is likely to cost something in the region of twenty four hundred pounds! One of the sought after prints in the book is the action between the Shannon and the Chesapeake and the plates depicting Nelson's victories are also in great demand. I managed to buy Plates I and II of Lord Howe's Victory, nicely framed, for forty pounds some few years ago and odd plates appear in the salerooms from time to time at not unreasonable prices.

Many of the maritime prints of the late 18th and early 19th century are now beyond the reach of the modest collector who should perhaps direct his interest to some of the delightful chromo-lithographs of the later Victorian period. There is a delightful three-volume work called *Her Majesty's Navy*, published about 1892, with excellent chromo-lithographs by Fred Mitchell and Christian Symons. A companion volume, *Her Majesty's Army*, contains military uniform prints of that period.

Thomas Whitcombe (c. 1760–c. 1824) appears to have been a prolific maritime painter working mainly in oils (but sometimes in watercolours) during the Napoleonic period; all the engravings in *Naval Achievements* are after paintings by him. He exhibited at the Royal Academy on some fifty-six occasions between 1783 and 1824 and his original oils now command high prices.

Process: Aquatint   Source: D. M. Beach, 1977

Size: 7″ by 10⅜″ (178 × 264mm)

Watermark: Whatman 1821

No. 53   Lord Howe's Victory June 1st, 1794, by Thomas Sutherland—aquatint *Author's Collection*

James Pollard 1792–1867

For a period of something like thirty years James Pollard painted and engraved the brightly coloured coaches of the Regency road and left behind an enduring legacy of interest and pleasure. Early issues of his coaching prints are now rare and costly, not least the ones produced before the year 1826 that were engraved by himself and published by the family firm of R. Pollard and Sons. The names of several important aquatint engravers are associated with Pollard's prints, including Robert Havell (Snr), Charles and George Hunt, R. G. Reeve and the Rosenberg family.

In 1815, Robert Pollard issued the first coaching prints of the series based on watercolour drawings prepared by his son James. These include one captioned *Stage Coach with the News of Peace* issued to celebrate the end of the war with France. The plate was re-issued in 1832 to mark the passing of the Reform Bill when the title of the print was changed to *Stage Coach with the News of Reform*. Another rare item is *Approach to Christmas* that was painted by Pollard and engraved by George Hunt. This print is undated but was published by J. Moore, possibly in the early 1830's.

There are six coaching prints in the collection, four by James Pollard all published by J. Watson, and two by Charles Cooper Henderson (1803–77) published by Ackermann. Henderson's coaching subjects are inclined to be larger than Pollard's and lacking in his primitive appeal. The popularity and high prices now being paid for early Pollard prints has produced the usual crop of reproductions and fakes. There is a gravure of *The General Post Office London* measuring $11\frac{1}{4}'' \times 16\frac{3}{4}''$ compared with the $16\frac{1}{2}'' \times 24\frac{3}{4}''$ of the original. There is also a lithographic copy of *Hyde Park Corner*, also much reduced and there are doubtless others. Some of Pollard's printing plates are still in existence, so there is unlikely to be any shortage of Pollard's in the salerooms for some time to come!

The print illustrated depicts the York and Edinburgh mailcoach heading north for Darlington and Durham, as indicated on the signpost. The print was published by J. Watson in 1826 and engraved by R. G. Reeve, although his name is incorrectly given on the print as G. Reeves. The companion plates in the collection are *The Mailcoach in a Drift of Snow* (1825), *The Mail Coach in a Thunder Storm on Newmarket Heath* (1827) and *The Mail Coach in a Flood* (1827). This latter print is beautifully hand coloured but the name of engraver F. Rosenberg is incorrectly spelt as F. Rosenbourg.

Process: Aquatint   Source: Private, 1973

Size: $10\frac{7}{8}'' \times 15\frac{7}{8}''$ (276 × 403mm)

Watermark: None

No. 54   The Mailcoach in a Storm of Snow after James Pollard—aquatint *Author's Collection*

James Duffield Harding 1797–1863

This important watercolour artist was born at Depford in 1797 and started his working life in a solicitor's office. His interest in art was doubtless aided by his father's influence and early training as a student of Paul Sandby. As a young man, James was awarded a Society of Arts medal for an original landscape and elected a member of the Water Colour Society.

He was one of the early pioneers of lithography in Britain and his early experimental work on stone was carried out in collaboration with Charles Hullmandel, a previous employee of Senefelder, inventor of the process.

One of my first Harding purchases as a somewhat inexperienced print collector was a lithographed view of *Barnbogle Castle* by J. D. Harding after Clarkson Stanfield. I was intrigued with the title of the print and the pair of sleepy fishermen dozing with their backs against a heavy, grounded fishing boat in the foreground. There is a restful simplicity about its composition that, of course, owes its origins to Stanfield not Harding. Harding seems at his best as a lithographer when he interprets the work of others.

I was later offered a copy of Harding's *Sketches at Home and Abroad* and found many of the plates lacking the Harding magic, although their worth today is probably due to their geographical locations rather than to any appreciation of Harding as a lithographer. Lovers of nature will be intrigued with *The Park and the Forest* with Harding's skilled renderings of trees and foliage, although these are more likely to be appreciated by the naturalist.

His view of High Street, Edinburgh, from the head of the West Bow after W. L. Leitch was one of many plates lithographed by Harding for an ambitious work *Scotland Delineated*, published between 1847–54. Many important artists contributed drawings, including J. M. W. Turner R.A., David Roberts R.A. and Clarkson Stanfield R.A., but the work did not achieve the commercial success it deserved. Plates from the series are not common and similar examples could well be costly.

Process: Lithograph

Source: Private, 1980

Size: $11\frac{1}{2}''\times 15\frac{3}{4}''$ (292 × 400mm)

Watermark: None

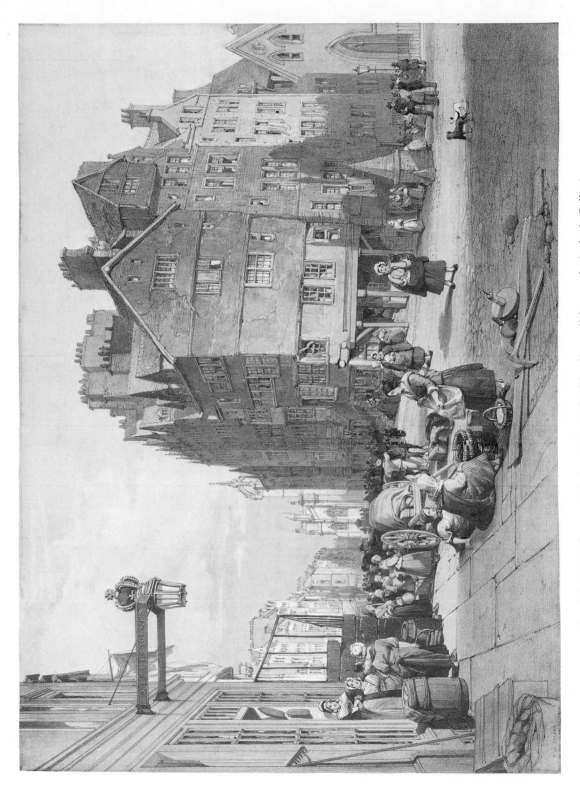

No. 55　High Street, Edinburgh by J. D. Harding—lithograph *Author's Collection*

Eugene Delacroix 1798–1863

The reader will have doubtless appreciated that apart from one or two notable exceptions this book concerns itself with native British traditions of print making. However, the contribution made by men like von Siegen, Le Prince and Senefelder to the development of the graphic arts is reflected in a great many of the prints that are illustrated here. Whilst the inventions of von Seigen and Le Prince are to do with print making techniques now largely forgotten, the process of lithography introduced by Senefelder is responsible for most of the world's present output of printed books and illustrations and therefore relates the past to the present in a very positive way.

Although French lithography developed in the 19th century with greater enthusiasm than in Britain, I have chosen to include this classic aquatint that I first saw illustrated in Alfred Whitman's *Print Collectors Handbook*. This important French painter and engraver enjoys a mere five lines in Slater's monumental work *Engravings and their Value*, despite Delacroix being regarded as the standard bearer of the Romantic movement who dominated the field of French painting in the 19th century.

As a rendering in pure aquatint, *Un Forgoron* provides dramatic treatment of light and shade and represents a refreshing departure from the traditional British use of this print process. Delacroix's artistic ability lifts the print above the mechanics of a print technique and it is unfortunate that modern printing processes do not enable it to be reproduced here with anything like the power and vigour of the original. One assumes that the original illustration in Whitman's book brought the print to the notice of a fairly wide readership but I have never seen another example and it would be interesting to know more about its origins.

A copy is listed in Slater as 'unfinished' and was priced at one pound, ten shillings in 1921. This example was purchased for very little more than that in 1970, when I was particularly concerned with researching the aquatint process. Since that time, a number of friendly dealers have attempted to buy the print and therein lies much of the interest and fascination of owning a rare and pleasing item.

Process: Pure aquatint   Source: Private, 1970

Size: $6\frac{1}{2}''\times 4''$ (165 × 102mm)

Watermark: None

152

No. 56   Un Forgoron by Eugene Delecroix—aquatint *Author's Collection*

David Lucas 1802–81

This large mezzotint plate of Constable's famous painting *The Lock* was scraped by David Lucas and published c. 1836. The two great landscape painters of the period, J. M. W. Turner and John Constable both concerned themselves with the issue of prints after their work. Turner claimed that he earned far more from the publishers of his prints than he did from the sale of his paintings but Constable's efforts in this field appear to have met with financial disaster.

The bulk of Turner's sketching and painting was line engraved by a veritable army of engravers, whereas Constable used David Lucas to render his work in mezzotint. Lucas printed his work at home and there appears to have been constant friction between the painter and himself; Constable claiming the mezzotints were too dark. Walter Thornbury highlights the difficulties in his book *The Life and Correspondence of J. M. W. Turner*. Writing of Lucas he says 'I knew David Lucas, the engraver, well. He was almost exclusively engraver to Constable; at least, Constable was out of temper if he took a plate from elsewhere. Always soaring to the unattainable, Constable was never satisfied with the plates; and after having once kept Lucas at alterations on a large plate (I think Salisbury Cathedral) his final exclamation was "Lucas, I only wish you could bring it to the state it was nine months ago"'

The partnership between Constable and Lucas led to the publication of *Various Subjects of Landscape* containing twenty two plates and published in parts between 1830–33. On the smaller prints the publisher's imprint reads 'London published by Mr. Constable, 35, Charlotte St., Fitzroy Square, 1830', although they were later re-issued without imprint (Plate 23). In 1845, some eight years after Constable's death, Lucas tried publishing a *New Series of Engravings of English Landscape*. Yet again, the venture failed, only now, with Constable dead, the cost of the project brought financial ruin to Lucas who tragically ended his days in a workhouse.

Another large mezzotint plate by Lucas, *The Cornfield*, is also in the collection. Both prints are without titles but are unlikely to be proofs before letters as the ruled borders are a little faint in parts. Both are printed on India paper and canvas backed. The prints were bought in Ludlow many years ago and are no doubt scarce, as I have never seen similar examples on offer since that time.

Process: Mezzotint/drypoint   Source: Bric-a-brac shop, Ludlow, 1975

Size: 22⅜″ by 19⅜″ (568 × 492mm)

Watermark: None

No. 57　The Lock by David Lucas—mezzotint *Author's Collection*

Thomas Sidney Cooper R.A., C.V.O.
1803–1902

This important Victorian animal painter has provided print collectors with a fine legacy of his lithographed work. In recent years there has been an increasing demand for his paintings and prints and the books containing his original lithographs have become scarce. His most famous publication is *Groups of Cattle Drawn from Nature*, printed by Hullmandel and published by Ackermann and Co., in 1839. The lithograph illustrated appeared in this work and is typical of Cooper's skill with animal studies and also demonstrates the ease and freedom with which he worked on the stone.

He was born in Canterbury in 1803 and experienced great poverty and hardship in early life. His youthful artistic ability was recognised by a local doctor, who was himself an amateur artist and did much to encourage Cooper's flair for drawing. On leaving school he obtained employment with a local coachbuilder and quickly mastered the techniques of coach painting. During the depression following the war with Napoleon's France he lost his employment but managed to secure an income by sketching and selling local views of Canterbury and by assisting the scene painter at the local theatre.

In 1827 Cooper decided to seek his fortune in France, where he became successful as an artist and earned a prosperous living as a drawing master. He later moved to Belgium, where he met and married Charlotte Pearson the daughter of an English Professor living there. Serious riots, followed by an invasion of Dutch troops and the loss of his brother-in-law in the fighting, brought Cooper and his family back to Britain in 1831.

His subsequent career as an animal painter can be traced to his lithographic work undertaken for Ackermann and he was to maintain his interest in this medium for the next twenty years. Cooper's earliest recorded work in lithography is a view of Canterbury Cathedral, published before his departure for France in 1820. Hullmandel also prepared *Views of Canterbury and its Environs*, six views lithographed by Cooper and published by Dickinson in 1827. There is a rare lithograph of the Coronation of William IV and Queen Adelaide, one of the first commissions undertaken by Cooper for Ackermann on his return to Britain. He exhibited at the Royal Academy on no less than two hundred and thirty different occasions and in 1901 his signal contribution to British painting was recognised when King Edward VII bestowed upon him the honour of the Royal Victorian Order. Cooper died on the 7th February, 1902 and was buried in the churchyard of St. Martin's, Canterbury.

Process: Lithograph—one tint-stone   Source: Private, 1970

Size: 11⅝″ by 18″ (294 × 458mm)   Watermark: None

No. 58   Animal Study by T. S. Cooper R.A.—lithograph *Author's Collection*

Thomas Shotter Boys 1803–74

On the 30th October, 1831, a serious fire broke out in the Armoury at the Tower of London. The fire raged unchecked for several days during which time 280,000 stand of arms and other equipment were destroyed. On the day following the outbreak Thomas Shotter Boys prepared and subsequently lithographed this historic, but somewhat uninteresting, plate which sadly displays little of the life and activity he was able to bring to *London as it Is* which he published some eleven years later in 1842.

This highly important lithographic work was printed by Hullmandel and consisted of some twenty-six views of London. A single tint-stone was employed together with hand colouring of outstanding quality. The originals were mounted on card and an issue was also available bound in book form with uncoloured plates. Prints from either work are now rare and costly. Shotter Boys also produced a series of lithographs on York (10 plates), some of the views having been prepared as early as 1837 although they were not issued until 1841, when they were published by Robert Sunter, bookseller of 23 Stonegate, York.

Boys was born at Pentonville, London in 1803 and apprenticed to George Cooke the engraver. Like T. S. Cooper, he spent much of his early career in France. On his return to Britain he produced lithographic works after a number of important contemporary artists including David Roberts (of Holy Land fame) and Clarkson Stanfield. Boys was one of a number of highly competent artists who realised that lithography provided an ideal medium with which to popularise their work by the issue of prints. Both J. D. Harding and Richardson of Newcastle stand very close to him, with their undoubted ability as topographical artists.

Some clever copies of *London as it Is* appeared on the market after the First World War, possibly produced from zinc plates, as were some of the America Yacht series. From the purely decorative standpoint, the excellent reproduction published by Traylen's, the Guildford Booksellers, offer an inexpensive and attractive alternative.

Process: Lithograph—one tint-stone   Source: Private, 1980

Size: 8″ × 16″ (203 × 407mm)

Watermark: None

No. 59   The Tower of London by Thomas Shotter Boys—lithograph *Author's Collection*

John Harris 1791–1873

British military prints, with their colourful uniforms and waving plumes, represent an aspect of print collecting so wide and varied that numerous books have been written on the subject. The nineteenth century was the great period of the British military print and one of the most prolific and famous aquatint engravers was John Harris, who engraved this fine example of the *Royal Artillery*, published by Rudolph Ackermann in 1855.

John Harris was the son of a famous father and clearly inherited his ability as a figure painter and engraver. His skills were widely used by the leading publishers of aquatint and any prints bearing his name are synonymous with high quality. He engraved works after James Pollard, Henry Alken and Cooper Henderson. Examples after these important painters are now rare and expensive and the Ackermann military prints particularly so.

The collector of military prints has a variety of choices open to him. He can collect uniform prints depicting the dress worn by the various regiments, or those depicting military exercises or tattoos. Military leaders have been represented by the printmakers in stipple, line, and mezzotint, with the lighter side of military life depicted by the work of Gillray, Rowlandson, Morland, Bunbury and Simkin. George Morland was naturally attracted to the less popular aspects of army life with his 'Deserter' series, engraved by George Keating. One of the less expensive kinds of reigmental print are those from *Her Majesty's Army*, a series of chromo-lithographs that include certain County regiments, Yeomanry and Colonial figure groups with particular emphasis on the Indian Regiments. The collected plates from this work were re-issued by Virtue in the early twentieth century as *British Imperial Forces*.

James Jenkins published his *Martial Achievements of Great Britain* in 1815 with some fifty odd, smallish aquatint pictures of battles engraved by Thomas Sunderland, Havell and Douberg and based on drawings by Heath, whose large plates are now rare and costly.

There are two excellent books on military costume. One is Ralph Nevill's *British Military Prints* published by *The Connoisseur* in 1909; the other W. Y. Carman's *British Military Uniforms*, published by Spring Books in 1960. The frontispiece of this book displays the first military print I bought and depicts the Scots Fusilier Guards outside Buckingham Palace, prior to their departure for the Crimea.

The Parker Gallery in London are the recognised international specialists for military prints but, sadly, the bulging folios of prints they were able to offer the collector some twenty years ago are now depleted.

Process: Etching and aquatint　　　　　　　　　　Source: Private, 1971

Size: 12″ × 8¾″ (304 × 222mm)

Watermark: None

160

No. 60   Royal Artillery by J. Harris—aquatint *Author's Collection*

Charles Eden Wagstaff 1805–1850

The great industrial and commercial expansion of Britain in the 19th century both at home and abroad provided exciting opportunities for the artists and print makers. The Victorians were great sightseers and the prints after Turner's drawings, coupled with the birth and rapid expansion of the railways, caught the public imagination and greatly encouraged people to travel. Two of the national highlights during the period were the Coronation and subsequent marriage of Queen Victoria to Prince Albert of Saxe-Coburg. The print illustrated is the latter of these two historically important events and was engraved after an original painting by Sir George Hayter (1792–1871).

They were published by Henry Graves in 1843 and 1844 respectively, the former being engraved by Henry Thomas Pyall (1811–67), although both Slater—*Engravings and their Value* and Rodney Engen—*Victorian Engravers and Print Publishers and their Works*, attribute it to Charles Wagstaff who engraved the example illustrated. Hayter was one of the leading portrait painters of the Victorian period and, despite many exhibitions at the Royal Academy and his important appointment as Painter of Historical Portraits to Her Majesty the Queen, he was never elected to membership. Hayter appears to have included himself in this painting and can be seen (lower right) on the print busily at work on what one assumes were his preliminary sketches for the painting that was intended to provide accurate portraits of the dignitaries present, photography being in its infancy. The victor of Waterloo is in the left background, his Field Marshal's baton gripped firmly in his right hand.

Many large engravings were produced during the later Victorian period. A number depict British Military victories abroad in India and Africa as the Empire was extended, whilst others portrayed expansion at home. *Derby Day* is possibly the best known, with Frith's *The Railway Station* (Victoria and Albert Museum) running a close second. Frith apparently used Paddington station as the subject for this painting, a busy platform scene with passengers, porters and a couple of top-hatted plain-clothes police about to handcuff a well dressed gentleman about to board the train. The locomotive is interesting and appears identical to the other Great Western engine depicted on the Bath Ford print.

I recollect buying both these prints some ten years ago for ten pounds but almost twenty times that sum would be needed to acquire them today. By contrast, the Coronation and Marriage prints were a gift. They were discovered by a local tradesman in the derelict outhouse of a property he had bought. Both were badly torn and covered with white-wash. Today, beautifully hand coloured and restored to their former glory, they are on loan to Lloyds Bank, a fitting tribute to the print specialist who restored them.

Process: Stipple and line engraving   Source: Private, 1973

Size: 22″ × 34″ (559 × 863mm)

Watermark: None

162

No. 61   The Marriage of Her Majesty Queen Victoria by C. E. Wagstaff—line engraving & stipple

Author's Collection

William Millington 1811–1890

One of my first art 'finds' in Wiltshire some fifteen years ago was a large watercolour of the Market Hall, Trowbridge, signed by a William Millington. I was unable to trace the artist in any of the standard reference books and subsequently sold the drawing to the local Council for very little more than the fifteen pounds I had paid for it. Some months later I saw a line engraving of *Trowbridge Castle* by this same William Millington and realised that I had sold an original item by an artist whose work had been engraved!

However, Millington has an ever greater claim to fame in the development of lithography in Britain by being one of the first provincial printers to use a Senefelder litho printing press (Plate 15). In 1835 he appears to have been employed by J. Hollway, a Bath printer of 10, Milsom Street, but within ten years of this date he was preparing and lithographing his own work. Its excellent quality must have been known to printers in the area, yet both the Tackle plate of *Bath Ford* and Isaac Ward's *Six Views of Devizes* were sent to London lithographers to be printed.

It would appear that Millington's graphic skills were not confined to his work as a lithographic artist. He painted in both oils and watercolours and taught drawing as well as being engaged as an architectural draughtsman. Two of the prints in the collection are lithographs of new buildings in Trowbridge, doubtless commissioned by the architects concerned. His print of the *National and Sunday Schools* (undated) carries the name of G. P. Manners, Architect, and his *New Alms Houses* (1860) that of H. Blandford, Architect.

The print of *Market-Place, Trowbridge*, is somewhat earlier, with the figures rather more primitive than on his later work. A single buff coloured tint-stone was used to good effect to highlight the cloud detail, the stonework of the steeple and the wall of the George Hotel. This particular print carries the sticker of a Glasgow Gilder and Picture Restorer verso so, clearly, Millington's work was known outside his native Wiltshire. I should be grateful to hear from anyone who can assist by providing information about any of his prints to enable details to be lodged with the Wiltshire County Records Office.

In 1903 Millington's historic press was purchased by the St. Bride Foundation Institute in London for the sum of five pounds. It is fortunate that it was photographed by Houlton Brothers of Trowbridge before leaving Wiltshire—... 'it is sad to record—this remarkable and almost certainly unique example of an early star-wheel press has since been lost or destroyed'—(Michael Twyman, *Journal of the Printing Historical Society* No. 3, 1967, pp. 3–50).

Process: Lithograph—one tint-stone   Source: Private, 1982

Size: $17\frac{3}{4}'' \times 12\frac{1}{2}''$ (450 × 318mm)

Watermark: None

No. 62 Market Place, Trowbridge by William Millington—lithograph
Author's Collection

Edward William Cooke R.A., F.R.S. 1811–80

This delightful print of an outward bound East Indiaman was etched by Edward William Cooke whilst still a boy in his teens. His painstaking attention to detail came to my notice many years ago on buying a print of a *Collier Discharging* from his first published series of *Fifty Plates of Shipping and Craft*, issued in 1828. A year later an enlarged book with an additional fifteen plates was issued as *Sixty-five plates of Shipping and Craft*.

Cooke apparently developed his great love of ships and the sea in his early teens and his undoubted artistic talent caused a Captain Burton to offer him a berth aboard the *Thetis*. This enabled him to study at first hand many of the sailing and steam vessels of the time. His marine etchings provide a valuable historical record of both sail and steam during this important period in Britain's development as a great maritime trading nation.

His etchings are still undervalued and this can only be due to the dimensions of the plates which are dwarfed by a Dutton in size, but not in quality. Many of the early issues were printed on India-paper and are usually foxed (spotted) when found today and so cannot be washed. There are some later impressions printed on a heavier paper that are quite satisfactory.

It seems that Cooke's genius as an etcher and marine painter received scant treatment from the art world until comparatively recently, despite the examples of his oils in the National Maritime Museum, the Tate Gallery and the Victoria and Albert Museum. Professor Arthur Hind's monumental *History of Engraving and Etching* makes no mention of him, nor does Alfred Whitman in his *Print Collector's Handbook*, although his father George Cooke, and uncle William B. Cooke, are both mentioned.

There are some excellent prints after Cooke in *Finden's Ports and Harbours*. This is usually found as a two volume work and was originally published by Charles Tilt in 1837. The titles to look for are *Yarmouth, Men of War at Spithead; Entrance to Portsmouth Harbour; View from the Saluting Platform, Portsmouth; Rigging Hulk and Frigate, Portsmouth; Gosport—Flag Ship Saluting*, and *Ramsgate*. Do not confuse the work of Edward William Cooke with that of his uncle W. B. Cooke, whose *Thames Scenery* published in 1818, is by comparison rather uninspiring.

Process: Original etching   Source: Warwick Leadlay Gallery, 1979

Size: $5\frac{5}{8}'' \times 7\frac{1}{8}''$ (429 × 181mm)

Watermark: None

No. 63 The Thames, East Indiaman by E. W. Cooke—etching *Author's Collection*

Thomas Goldsworth Dutton c. 1816–78

Very little appears to be known about the early life of this famous 19th century maritime watercolourist and lithographer whose prints are now in great demand. There is some evidence of Dutton having received early training as a wood engraver but the bulk of his lithographic work was based on drawings made by himself. He was possibly the most prolific of all 19th century maritime artists and his subjects cover most of the naval and commercial shipping of the busy Victorian era.

The clipper ship 'Lincolnshire' is a recent addition to the collection and was built by the famous Blackwall firm of Money Wigram. The clipper is flying the house flag of Green and Wigram and therefore the print must have been made before this partnership was dissolved in 1843. Early in the partnership no decision had been taken with regard to a house flag and the enterprising Mr. Green decided that a square flag of St. George would be an excellent choice. On taking delivery of a new vessel he sailed into port proudly flying the flag atop his mainmast. The port admiral was not amused to see his personal flag flying from a merchantman and a red faced Mr. Green was confronted by a very irrate senior naval gentleman!

The flag was lowered as requested but the enterprising Mr. Green was not to be outdone and a blue square of material was promptly pinned to both sides of the flag and immediately re-hoisted. This house flag remained in use until the partnership of Green and Wigram was dissolved many years later, when Green superimposed the red cross over the blue background for his new line.

Many of these vessels were engaged in the tea trade with the Far East, whilst others were used for the opium traffic between India and China. Tea was a precious commodity in Victorian Britain and in important households the tea-caddy was kept permanently locked with the key in the possession of the Housekeeper.

For the reader anxious to see more of Dutton's work there is a fine collection in the National Maritime Museum at Greenwich and some excellent colour postcards of the vessels he depicted. For the collector seeking original Dutton lithographs I can offer little hope. When his prints appear on the market today they are likely to command prices that are far beyond the reach of the modest collector.

Process: Lithograph—one tint-stone   Source: Private, 1983

Size: 12″ × 18″ (304 × 458mm)

Watermark: None

168

No. 64 The 'Lincolnshire' by T. G. Dutton—lithograph *Author's Collection*

H. Guest fl. 1840–53

In 1828 Lord Lansdowne's Act made it a capital offence to shoot at another man with intent to kill, maim, or do him grievous bodily harm. In 1837 the law was amended and, providing no blood was shed, the treadmill or transportation for life were the attractive alternatives! A great many famous and important people appear to have escaped the law with regard to duelling, including the Duke of Wellington, Lord Castlereagh, the fifth Lord Byron, The Duke of York and Lord Cardigan. It is possible that this print was published about 1840 and was issued by the proprietor of Mardon's Shooting Gallery of 94 Pall Mall, in order to popularise his establishment.

This rare print is the most recent acquisition to the collection but has defied all efforts to trace its publisher or origins. Very little more is known about the artist or engraver concerned, although Graves lists a Thomas Kearnan working in London between 1821–50 who exhibited landscapes at the Royal Academy on two occasions. He was also responsible for engraving two plates for *The Royal Pavilion at Brighton* (J. Nash, 1826) and four for Brayley's *Antiquities of the Priory of Christ-church* (1834).

Guest is also listed by Graves as having worked in London between 1843 and 1853 and he appears to have been a portrait painter of some merit, exhibiting three times at the Royal Academy. There is a print of Deer Stalking after C. Hancock by him. The aquatint quality of this print is outstanding and other examples of work in aquatint by Guest must surely exist for his skill to have developed in this way.

Quite apart from the dress of the period, the print provides interesting play-bill information on the Theatre Royal, Covent Garden and a reference to Fanny Kemble. Kean in Richard III is at the Theatre Royal, Drury Lane, and there is a Coronation Fete at Vauxhall Gardens, doubtless celebrating the accession of Queen Victoria. Champagne for the occasion could have been bought for '63s per dozen'.

Today, the site of No. 94 Pall Mall is owned by the Royal Automobile Club and is at present undergoing major repairs and rennovation. I had hoped to visit the premises to ascertain whether the indoor achitecture of the room illustrated was the same today as when the print was made but the original building is no longer in existence.

Process: Etching/aquatint   Source: Private, 1983

Size: $8\frac{1}{2}'' \times 12\frac{3}{8}''$ (215 × 314mm)

Watermark: None

170

No. 65   Mardon's Shooting Gallery by H. Guest—aquatint *Author's Collection*

William Simpson (War artist) 1824–99

In 1855 Paul and Dominic Colnaghi and Co., of London published a large folio volume with the title *The Seat of the War in the East,* containing some sixty lithographs in colour based on drawings by William Simpson, a young Scot from Glasgow. Simpson had trained as a lithographer in Scotland and on arrival in London quickly found employment with Day and Son, the Queen's Printer.

His 'on the spot' drawings of the Crimean War resulted from an agreement made between his employer, William Day, and the eventual publisher of the work, Messrs Colnaghi, although Simpson had been told in no uncertain terms that his travelling expenses to reach the theatre of war was entirely his own affair! On his arrival in the Crimea the tragedy of the ill-fated Charge of the Light Brigade was uppermost in the minds of the troops, the disaster having taken place only three weeks previously. Twice Simpson submitted sketches of the action to Lord Cardigan and twice the Light Brigade commander rejected these out of hand. Simpson decided he would make a third attempt after which he would send the drawings to London, whether Lord Cardigan approved or not. On this occasion he depicted Cardigan ahead of the charging cavalry and his Lordship was delighted.

It is interesting to speculate why Simpson did not show Lord Cardigan leading the charge in his first two drawings, for he surely based these on accounts of survivors and eye witnesses. 'The controversy over the Earl of Cardigan's behaviour during the charge raged on for years; eight years later he was still suing a Colonel Calthorpe for libel contained in a book the colonel had published...' (see *The Crimea Blunder*—Peter Gibbs, Muller, London 1960).

The Simpson plates are of great interest to today's military historian. Those most in demand are the *Charge of the Light Cavalry Brigade* (illustrated) *and the Charge of the Heavy Cavalry,* lead by the Scots Greys. One print of a ward in the Hospital of Scutari is said to depict Florence Nightingale ministering the wounded, although she is not mentioned by name in the accompanying text. These three plates are somewhat scarce and expensive but others from the series may still be purchased for a few pounds.

Process: Lithography—two tint-stones   Source: Private, 1980

Size: $10\frac{3}{4}'' \times 18\frac{3}{4}''$ (273 × 477mm)

Watermark: None

172

No. 66 Charge of the Light Cavalry Brigade after William Simpson—lithograph *Author's Collection*

Myles Birket Foster R.W.S. 1825–99

Myles Birket Foster was born in North Shields in February, 1825, the youngest of five brothers in a family of staunch northern Quakers. The household moved to London in 1830 and Myles was eventually employed by Ebenezer Landells, a Newcastle man who had been a pupil of Thomas Bewick. Foster's natural talent for drawing was quickly recognised by his employer and for some five years the young artist was engaged in the preparation of drawings on wood blocks that were subsequently engraved for the books and leading magazines of the day.

In 1848 Foster joined his friend Edmund Evans in a wood engraving business that specialised in providing the illustrated block-work for the *London Illustrated News*. There was an increasing demand for his services as a book illustrator and for about seven years Foster produced the illustrations and Evans engraved the blocks. Throughout this period the artist had been developing his skills as a painter in watercolours and in 1860 he was elected an Associate of the Water Colour Society.

In 1866 he visited Venice and this was followed by a series of European tours. The drawings he prepared were then reproduced as line and wood engravings in many of the books of the period. The bulk of his watercolour work is on board and inclined to be small, displaying a remarkable amount of detail and a 'featherlike' quality that suggests the use of fine brushes and a dry, almost stipple-like application of watercolour.

The popularity of Birket Foster's watercolours provided great scope for the chromo-lithographers of the late 19th century. The example illustrated was reproduced by this process and is considerably larger than the original watercolour that measures a mere six inches by eight and three-quarter inches. These chromo-lithographic copies of Foster's work still appear in the sale rooms from time to time and may easily be mistaken for watercolours. The forger usually overpaints the monogram of the artist's initials in red, because this is the only portion of the print that betrays the fact that the item has been printed.

The late chromo-lithographic prints of the 19th century are gaining in popularity with collectors because of their remarkable quality. Of these the Pear's Soap series are possibly the best known but readers are reminded that many reproductions exist, all of which are likely to display the 'dotted' pattern employed by modern colour printing processes.

Process: Chromo-lithograph   Source: Bath Antique Market, 1980

Size: 7″ × 10″ (178 × 254mm)

Watermark: None

No. 67   The Toy Boat by Miles B. Foster R.W.S.—chromo-lithograph *Author's Collection*

Thomas Picken fl. 1837–d. 1870

This important Victorian artist and lithographer worked for the early established lithographic printers Messrs Day and Haghe. Upon the death of William Day in 1845, the name of the firm changed to Day and Son and as this undated lithograph of Bath Ford carries the Day and Son imprint, it must have been published in 1845, or later. The print is a typical example of important work that was sketched locally and then lithographed in London on behalf of provincial clients.

The lithographer Thomas Picken is known to have worked for Day and Haghe and was still working for Day and Son in 1854. After exhibiting at the Royal Academy in 1857 he emigrated to Australia, where he died in 1870. His work as a lithographer is well known to collectors and dealers and is inclined to command high prices. Apart from individual lithographs, Picken produced plates for a number of important works, including *The Queen's visit to Jersey* (1847), Walker's views of *The Principal Buildings in London* (1852), Roberts' *Holy Land* (1855) and Pyne's *Landscape Scenery* (1859).

The print makers have provided us with an interesting pictorial record of the development of the railway system and whilst some early prints were produced in aquatint, the vast majority were black and white lithographs that were subsequently hand coloured. The most famous series of railway prints are the aquatints printed in colour after Thomas Talbot Bury that were published on *The London and Birmingham Railroad* in 1837. Some two years later John Cooke Bourne's lithographs, *Drawings of the London and Birmingham Railway*, were published and in 1846 Bourne issued his mammoth work *The History and Description of the Great Western Railway*.

Some early print-books of the railway era are now scarce and expensive:

1831 *Six Coloured Views on the Liverpool and Manchester Railway*	T. T. Bury
1831 *Views of the Most Interesting Scenery on the Line of the Liverpool and Manchester Railway*	J. Shaw
1831 *An Account of the Liverpool & Manchester Railway*	H. Booth
1845 *Views on the Manchester and Leeds Railway*	A. F. Tait
Ireland	
1834 *Five Views on the Dublin and Kingstown Railway*	A. Nicholl
1834 *Thirteen Views on the Dublin and Kingstown Railway*	R. Clayton
1836 *Six Views on the Dublin and Drogheda Railway*	J. E. Jones
Scotland	
1832 *Views of the Opening of the Glasgow and Garnkirk Railway*	D. O. Hill

Process: Lithograph—one tint-stone   Source: Private, 1978

Size: $12\frac{3}{4}'' \times 18\frac{1}{8}''$ (324 × 460mm)   Watermark: None

176

No. 68   Bath Ford by Thomas Picken—lithograph *Author's Collection*

Mrs Jane Wells Loudon 1807–58

Today's interest in floral art has produced a demand for flower and botanical plates for decorative purposes and the latter are enjoying a particular vogue in the United States at the present time. Many of the fine floral and botanical plate books of the 18th and 19th century were produced in etch, stipple and aquatint and are now keenly sought by collectors. The Victorian young lady of means was encouraged to draw and paint and many of the scrapbooks of that period testify to the excellence of some of their work.

The marriage to John Claudius Loudon, the botanist, was to result in the publication of a number of important flower books based on drawings and lithographs made by his wife Jane Wells Loudon. Between 1840 and 1848 this industrious and talented lady produced no less than five important illustrated works, the first of which was *The Ladies Flower Garden of Ornamental Annuals* containing forty eight hand coloured plates and published in 1840. *The Ladies Flower Garden of Bulbous Plants* followed in 1841, with fifty eight plates, and in 1843/4 a more voluminous work with ninety six coloured plates. *The Ladies Flower Garden of Ornamental Perennials*. The print illustrated is taken from *British Wild Flowers*, published in 1856, and containing sixty one plates of some three hundred species. Despite a second edition in 1849, this work appears to be quite rare and several hundred pounds would be needed to buy it today. Mrs Loudon's other important work *The Ladies Flower Garden of Ornamental Greenhouse Plants*, with forty two colour plates, was published in 1848.

The most popular plates sought by present day enthusiasts are orchids and roses. Many of the later Victorian flower prints produced by chromo-lithography are still quite cheap to buy. There is an excellent series that was issued in *The Garden* and with careful searching may still be bought for pence rather than pounds, although some examples are badly cropped. The choice of a suitable mount and carefully matched frame can result in prints of great beauty and decorative appeal.

For the reader wishing to make a serious study of flower plates, Alice M. Coats *Book of Flowers*, published by Phaidon in 1973, traces the development of flower books from the earliest times to the close of the nineteenth century.

Process: Hand coloured lithograph   Source: Lacy Gallery, 1980

Size: $10\frac{1}{2}''$ × 9″ (267 × 229mm)

Watermark: None

Pl. 34

1 *Burnet Rose* 2 *Sweet Briar, or Eglantine* 3 *Common Dog Rose* 4 *Ayrshire Rose*

No. 69   Wild Flowers by Mrs Loudon—lithograph *Author's Collection*

Carlo Pellegrini fl. 1860

This famous Victorian magazine was founded by Thomas Gibson Bowles and commenced publication in the autumn of 1868. In January of 1869 the magazine carried a caricature of Mr. Disraeli prepared by 'Ape' (Carlo Pellegrini) and established a tradition of weekly cartooning and lampooning that was to continue until the outbreak of war in 1914.

For something like forty-five years a steady stream of famous and infamous personalities enlivened the weekly issues of *Vanity Fair*, each in their turn to be battered or acclaimed by the pen of Jehu Junior, originally the pseudonym of the magazine's owner, T. G. Bowles. A great many of the cartoons were the work of 'Spy' (Leslie Ward), whose subjects included Royalty, judges, politicians, criminals, sportsmen, artists, actors and musicians of Victorian and later, Edwardian Britain.

The prints were produced in colour by chromo-lithography by Vincent Brooks, Day and Son, and their soft tonal quality cannot be bettered by any of today's modern printing techniques.

The caricature of the Marquis of Bath bears the caption 'Ancient lineage' and Jehu Junior comments in support as follows:

'The Thynnes have been a family rich enough to be called good for nigh upon four hundred years, and they are of the few whose titular nobility dates from the time of the Tudors. Nevertheless, they procured for themselves from the House of Brunswick a marquisate which descended in a direct line upon its present possessor, when he was but a boy of six years. He has lived up to the traditions imposed by ancient lineage and displayed all the respect due to the position derived from it. Exceptionally well looking as a youth, the ladies became addicted to him, and he naturally devoted himself to pleasure. Yet it is not recorded of him that he ever in its pursuit overstepped the bounds of honour, or ever forgot that he was a gentleman. He once belonged to a famous Navigator, but having left his ship without leave and married himself out of discipline, he has of late taken a share of business in the House of Lords, being moved thereto by an inborn courage and a lively apprehension of the blatant and lusty Democracy which he sees ready to devour marquises together with all other established powers. He is a very decent man, of whom good would be spoken even if he were a common person by those from whom his qualities might obtain notice; and he is so modest as to believe in his order even in preference to himself.'

For the collector starting late, the delights of Vanity Fair cartoons have much to offer, not least their reasonable impact on the pocket!

Process: Chromo-lithograph   Source: Suckling, 1976

Size: 12⅛″ × 7¼″ (308 × 184mm)

Watermark: None

No. 70   The Marquis of Bath by Carlo Pellegrini—chromo-lithograph
Author's Collection

Some Representative Cricketers 'Graphic' 1890

Tucked away in the archives at Cambridge House there is an early 19th century lithograph titled *The Village Green*, depicting groups of happy children at play. Some eight different games and pastimes are represented including cricket where the umpire is wearing a smock and the wicket-keeper a top hat! Cricket is also represented in one of a series of Ackermann lithographs, *Six Views in Devizes*, published by Isaac Ward in the middle 1840's and not included in Abbey's important work on lithography and aquatint. Here too, a cricket match is in progress on the Green, proof (if any were needed) of how well our national game was established in the early nineteenth century.

The middle years of the century were to provide the great cricket prints produced mainly by the lithographic process—sometimes in both lithography and line engraving as the 'portraiture' print of Sussex v. Kent at Brighton after Drummond and published in 1849, depicting a match that never took place! Frequently, as with the print just mentioned, local topography was incorporated into prints to provide wider customer appeal. Most cricket prints fall into two categories, either matches in progress, or single figure studies of the important personalities of the game, of which the '*Sketches at Lords*' series is probably the best known. The single figure tradition was continued by Carlo Pellegrini and Leslie Ward with their *Vanity Fair* cartoons that include the Hon. Alfred Lyttleton, Dr. W. G. Grace, and Ranjitsinhji. There was a fine series of single figure studies produced on green backgrounds by Eyre and Spottiswoode. Both these and the 'Spy' cartoons of cricketers are now very difficult to find, despite their somewhat recent origins. Years ago I bought 'W.G.' from Sucklings shop in Cecil Court, London, where the print was pinned to the woodwork of the shop-door, priced at seven shillings and sixpence! I rather think that anything less than twenty pounds would not buy him today.

Some Representative Cricketers was amongst a bundle of prints acquired cheaply many years ago when it was my custom to pass to my brother any cricket prints that came my way (he being badly afflicted with the cricket bug!). I was so fascinated at the engraver's skill in producing so many excellent portraits on wood that I decided to include the item in the collection, proof that in print collecting, as in life, the best things are often free.

Process: Wood engraving   Source: Private, 1972

Size: 15″ × 23¼″ (381 × 591mm)

Watermark: None

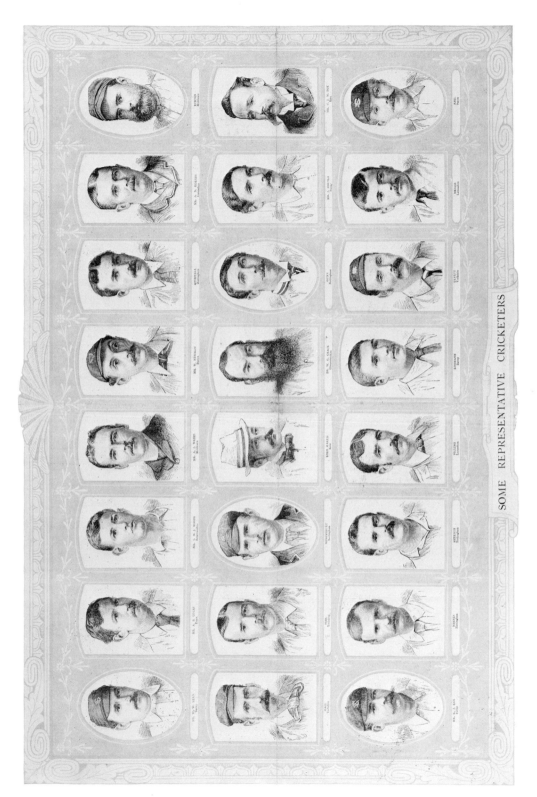

SOME REPRESENTATIVE CRICKETERS

No. 71   Some Representative Cricketers—'Graphic' 1890—wood engraving

Terms used in print collecting

AD VIVUM
Meaning *from the life*, usually follows the name of the engraver indicating that the portrait was taken from a sitter not a painting. William Hogarth's print of Lord Lovat (Plate 20) is one such example.

AFTER
Indicates that an engraving was *after* (or copied from) the work of someone else, i.e. David Lucas *after* John Constable. The term *by and after* indicates that the original work and the print were by the same person.

AQUATINT
A method of using acid to bite a design on a metal plate on which has been deposited a resin ground.

ARTIST'S PROOF
A print signed by the artist signifying to the engraver that it is a satisfactory representation of the artist's original painting or drawing.

BLOCK
A term originally used for the blocks used by wood engravers. Used today to describe any illustrated printing plate.

BURIN
Another name for a graver, the tool used to incise line engraved plates.

BURR
Term for the metal displaced when incising a metal plate and not usually removed when undertaking drypoint work.

BURNISHER
An engraving tool used to 'rub out' engraved lines.

CIRCA
Usually abbreviated to c. meaning 'about'.

CHIAROSCURO
The imposition of two or more blocks or plates by which means independent effects of light and shade may be produced.

CHALCOGRAPHY
To engrave on metal plates.

CROSS-HATCHING
Criss-crossed engraved lines used to produce darker areas on prints—the engraver's method of producing shading.

CRADLE OR ROCKER
Tool used in mezzotint process to 'plough up' the surface of the metal plate in order to lay the mezzotint ground.

CROPPED
A print that has been trimmed, sometimes with the loss of some of the engraved surface.

DELINEAVIT
From the Latin 'he drew it' from a drawing—or Pinxit from a painting.

ENGRAVER'S PROOFS
Print pulled from the plate as the work of engraving proceeds and used by both engraver and artist to assess the work.

ETCHING
A method of incising metal by means of acid applied through a wax ground.

ETCHING NEEDLE
The tool used by an etcher to prepare a design on metal.

EXECUDIT
He did it—usually follows the engraver's name on a print.

FECIT
The same as the previous term—frequently used by Hollar.

Fl.
Flourished.

FOXING
Spots or stains on prints usually caused by damp.

GRAVER
Tool used by the engraver to incise lines on metal.

GROUND
Term used in mezzotint, etching and aquatint for the preparation of the plate prior to engraving or etching.

INTAGLIO
Pronounced in-tal-i-ow—to incise, a plate where the printing surface is below the top of the plate.

INDIA PAPER
A very fine, silky paper capable of producing fine impressions when printed on and usually reserved for early pulls from the plate.

LAID-DOWN
Prints that have been pasted to a paper, card or canvas backing. Many valuable 19th century prints were laid down on canvas stretchers. Attempts to soak them off often causes the prints to crack.

LINE ENGRAVING
Method of incising lines on metal by means of a graver or burin.

LITHOGRAPH
Originally a print taken off a drawing made on limestone. Stones were replaced by metal (usually zinc) plates in latter period of 19th century.

MARGINS
The unprinted area surrounding a print—often minimal on early examples of old prints.

MEZZOTINT
Engraving process mainly developed for portraiture in the 17th century and much practiced in Britain.

PROOF
An early impression taken when the plate was in pristine condition.

PLATE
Used to describe an illustrated item as well as a printing-plate.

PINXIT
Usually follows the artist's name on a print indicating that the item was reproduced from a painting as opposed to a drawing.

PLANOGRAPHIC
A method of surface printing, i.e. lithography.

PRINT
An inked impression made on paper, silk or other suitable material from a hand worked block, plate or stone.

RELIEF PRINT
A print made from a raised printing surface, i.e. wood engraving.

REMARQUE
A small design usually inserted beneath the print in the lower paper margin. Popular with certain etchers in the late 19th century. Often used by Cecil Aldin who used a fox or hounds on his sporting prints.

RULING MACHINE

A device used in the nineteenth century to mechanically rule in the sky detail and similar areas. A fine steel comb used through a wax ground produces a similar effect.

SCULPSIT

Usually follows the engraver's name on a print—he engraved it.

STIPPLE

A method of engraving by means of dots.

STATE

Denotes the various alterations made to a plate after the original printing. Applies particularly to old master prints, etchings and mezzotints.

XYLOGRAPH

An engraving on wood or a print from the same.

Bibliography

Abbey, J. R.   *Scenery of Britain and Ireland in Aquatint and Lithography*. 1952

Allen, Brian   *Print Collecting*. 1970

Arlot, John & Daley, Arthur   *Pageantry of Sport*. 1968

Baily, Herbert   *George Morland*. 1906

Bedford, John   *Victorian Prints*. 1969

Booth, John   *Looking at Old Maps*. 1979

Calloway, Stephen   *English Prints for the Collector*. 1981

Carduss, N. & Arlott, J.   *The Noblest Game*. 1969

Darby, M.   *Early Railway Prints H.M.S.O.* 1974

Engen, R. K.   *Dictionary of Victorian Engravers, Print Publishers and their Works*. 1979

Godfrey, Richard   *Printmaking in Britain*. 1978

Graves, A.   *A Dictionary of Artists and Engravers*. 1901 (Reprinted)

Gray, Basil   *The English Print*. 1937

Hardie, Martin   *English Coloured Books*. 1906

Hayden, Arthur   *Chats on Old Prints*

Hind, Arthur M.   *A History of Engraving and Etching*. 1908 (Reprinted)

Hughes, Thurle   *Prints for the Collector*. 1970

Hunnisett, B.   *A Dictionary of British Steel Engravers*. 1980

Johnson, Peter   *Front Line Artists*. 1978

Nevill, Ralph   *British Military Prints*. 1909

Nevill, Ralph   *Old Sporting Prints*. 1908 (Reprinted)

Rees, Gareth   *Early Railway Prints*. 1980

Siltzer, Frank   *The Story of British Sporting Prints*. 1920 (Reprinted)

Shaw-Sparrow, W.   *British Etching*, 1926; *British Sporting Artists.* 1922 (Reprinted)

Slater, J. Herbert   *Engravings and their Value.* 1921 (Reprinted)

Tannahill, Reay   *Regency England (Colour prints).* 1964

Thornbury, Walter   *The Life and Correspondence of J. M. W. Turner* (reprinted)

Tooley, R. V.   *English Books with Colour Plates.* 1973

Wardroper, John   *The Caricatures of George Cruikshank.* 1977

Wedmore, F.   *Fine Prints.* 1910

White, Gleeson   *English Illustration (1855–70).* 1897 (Reprinted)

Whitman, Alfred   *The Print Collector's Handbook.* 1901 (Reprinted)

Wilder, F. L.   *How to Identify Old Prints.* 1969

U.K. Dealers in Old Prints

J. Ash (Rare Books)
25 Royal Exchange, London, EC3.
Tel. 01 626 2665

Barnard Gallery
Grange Farm, Brewer Lane, Everton, Doncaster.
Tel. 0777 817324

Edgar Backus Ltd.
44–46 Cank Street, Leicester, LE1 5GU.
Tel. 0533 58137

D. M. Beach
52 High Street, Salisbury, Wilts. SP1 2PG.
Tel. 0722 3801

B & B Gallery
15 George Street, Warminster, Wilts.
Tel. 0985 215413

Benet Gallery
18, King's Parade, Cambridge.
Tel. 0223 353783

T. J. Booth OBE
Surrey Maps and Prints, 'Manston', 33 Beaconsfield Road, Claygate, Esher, Surrey
Tel. 0372 62764

Paul Breen (Fine Art) Ltd.
The Lyver Gallery, 8 Hackins Hey, Dale Street, Liverpool, Merseyside, L2 2AW.
Tel. 051 236 7524

Brobury House Gallery
Brobury, Herefordshire.
Tel. 09817 229

Burlington Gallery
10 Burlington Gardens, London, W1X 1LG.
Tel. 01 734 9228

Cartographia Ltd.
Covent Garden, 37, Southampton St, London WC2E 7HE.
Tel. 01-240 568718

H. G. Chapman
86 Upper St. Giles Street, Norwich, Norfolk, NR2 1LT.
Tel. 0603 661837

Channel Islands Galleries Ltd.	Island Craft Centre, Trinity Square, St. Peter Port, Guernsey, Channel Islands. Tel. 0481 23247
Collectors Treasures Ltd.	Hogarth House, High Street, Wendover, Bucks. HP22 6DU. Tel. 0296 624402
	91 High Street, Amersham, Bucks. HP7 0DU. Tel. 024 03 7213
Dorchester Galleries	Rotten Row, Dorchester on Thames, Oxon. OX9 8LJ. Tel. 0865 341116
D. G. & A. S. Evans	7 The Struet, Brecon, LD3 7LL. Tel. 0874 2714
Fores Gallery Ltd.	Potterspury House, Potterspury, Towcester, Northants
Betty Haslam	4 Market Place, Faringdon, Oxon. Tel. 0367 21574
Hampshire Bookshop	Kingsgate Arch, Winchester, Hants. SO23 9PD. Tel. 0962 64710
John & Judith Head	Barn Book Supply, 88 Crane Street, Salisbury, Wilts. Tel. 0722 27767
Heritage Books Ltd.	7 Cross Street, Ryde, I.O.W., PO332 2AD. Tel. 0983 62933
Julia Holmes	Muirfield Place, Bunch Lane, Haslemere, Surrey. Tel. 0428 2153
J. Alan Hulme	The Old Map and Print Gallery, 54 Lower Bridge Street, Chester. Tel. 0244 44006
Ingol Maps and Prints	Cantsfield House, 206 Tag Lane, Ingol, Preston, Lancashire, PR2 3TX. Tel. 0772 724769

192

Lacy Gallery	38 Ledbury Road, London, W11 2AB. Tel. 01-229 9105
Leadenhall Gallery	6 Pudding Lane, Maidstone, Kent. Tel. 0622 683707
Litchfield Gallery	1062 Christchurch Road, Boscombe, Bournemouth, Dorset, BH7 6DS. Tel. 0202 425424
Lott and Gerrish Ltd.	14 Mason's Yard, Duke St., St. James, London, SW1Y 6BU. Tel. 01 930 1353
	The Old Rectory, Froxfield, Marlborough, Wiltshire. Tel. 0488 82188
G. & D. I. Marrin & Sons.	149 Sandgate Road, Folkestone, Kent. CT21 2DA. Tel. 0303 53016
Map House of London	54 Beauchamp Place, Knightsbridge. London. SW3 1NY. Tel. 01 589 4325/9821
John O. Nelson	22–24 Victoria Street, Edinburgh, EH1 2JN. Tel. 225 4413
O'Shea Gallery	6 Ellis Street (Off Sloane St.), Belgravia, London, SW1 9AL. Tel. 01-730 0081/2
Oldfield Antique Maps & Prints	34 Northam Road, Southampton, Hampshire, SO2 0PA. Tel. 0703 38916
Parker Gallery	12A–12B Berkeley Street, London, W1X 5AD. Tel. 01 499 5906/7
Paul Mason Gallery	149 Sloane Street, London, SW1X 9BZ. Tel. 01 730 3683

Petersfield Bookshop	16a, Chapel Street, Petersfield, Hants. GU32 3DS. Tel. 0730 63438
Pierpoint Gallery	10 Church Street, Hereford, HR1 2LR. Tel. 0432 267002
Printed Page	2–3 Bridge Street, Winchester, Hampshire. Tel. 0962 54072
Jean Pain	34 Trinity Street, Cambridge. Tel. 0223 358279
Jonathan Potter Ltd.	No. 1 Grafton Street, London, W1X 3LB. Tel. 01 491 3520
John Roberts Bookshop A.B.A.	43 Triangle West, Clifton, Bristol, BS8 1ES. Tel. 0272 28568
Robert Douwma Prints & Maps Ltd.	4 Henrietta Street, Covent Garden, London, WC2 8QU. Tel. 01 836 0771
C. Samuels & Sons Ltd.	17/18 Waterbeer Street (Guildhall Centre), Exeter, Devon EX4 3EH. Tel. 0392 73219
Stable Antiques	14 Loughborough Road, Hoton, Leics. LE12 5SF. Tel. (0509) 880208
Taurus Gallery	5 Wadham Road, Putney, London, SW15 2LS. Tel. 01 874 2534
Traylen's	Castle House, 49–50 Quarry Street, Guildford, Surrey, GU1 3UA. Tel. 0483 572424
Tudor Rose Antiques	31/32 Castle Street, Beaumaris, Anglesey, Gwynedd, LL58 8EE. Tel. 0248 810203
Warwick Leadlay Gallery	5 Nelson Road, Greenwich, London, SE10 9JB. Tel. 01 858 0317

Waterloo Fine Arts Ltd.	Penthouse, Calcot Grange, Mill Lane, Reading, RG3 5RS. Tel. 0734 411706
Walton, L	41 Woodland Road, Levenshulme, Manchester, M19 2GW. Tel. 061 224 6630
Welbeck Gallery	18 Thayer Street, London, W1M 5LD. Tel. 01 935 4825
West Gate Fine Art	16 St. Peter's Street, Canterbury, Kent. CT1 2BQ. Tel. 0227 53636
Witch Ball Print Shop	48 Meeting House Lane, Brighton, BN1 1HB. Tel. 02731 26618
Zwan Antiques	19 West Street, Dunster, Somerset, TA24 6SN. Tel. 064 382 657

Index

A General History of Quadrupeds
  (Bewick 1790)   39
Ackermann   112, 118, 140, 142, 148, 156, 182
Admiral   168
Aesops Fables   30
Alken, H.   37, 38, 79, 93, 142
Alken, S.   142
American Philosophical Society   75
American Volumatic Marker   87
Amiens   132
Amlwch Harbour   130, 131
Amsterdam   140
Angling   128, 134
Antique Print   21
Antwerp   96
'Ape' (Carlo Pellegrini)   180, 182
Appleton, T.   114
Aquafortis   57
Aquatint   21, 34, 36, 37, 55, 57, 58, 70, 112
   128, 130, 142, 148, 152, 160, 182
Archival Aids   85
Armada—Spanish   25
Art Reference Books   88, 89, 90
Arundel, Earl of   26, 29
Asperne, J.   126
Atlas of England and Wales (Saxton)   23
Australia   140, 176
A Voyage Round Great Britain (Daniell)   130
Aylesbury   100

Barlow   30, 31
Barnard, W.   124
Barnbogle Castle   150
Baron, B.   98
Barraud, W. & H.   90, 91
Bartolozzi, F.   34, 55, 56, 114
Basle   134
Bath   108, 144, 162, 164, 176
Bath, Marquis of   180, 181
BBC   76, 88
Baxter, G.   42, 43, 67, 68, 69, 71, 124
Beaufort, Duke A.   90
Becket, I.   33
Beer Street—Hogarth   98
Belgium   156
Benlowes *Theophila*   30
'Ben-Tally-Ho'   40, 142
Berlin   140
Berwick-upon-Tweed   110

Bewick   34, 38, 61, 174
Birds of Australia (Gould)   102
Birds of Europe (Gould)   102
Birds of Great Britain (Gould)   102
Birmingham   176
Biting (Acid)   28, 57
Blackwall   168
Blaeu   27, 48
Blandford, H.   164
Blome, R.   30, 31
Board of Ordnance   106
Bohn   116
Bologna   22
Bolsover   96
Bolton Bridge   132
Book Auction Records   75, 89, 90
Book of British Etching from Barlow to
   Seymour Haden   104
Booth, J.   138, 139
Booths *Australia*   140
Bosse, A.   46
Boston Public Library   122
Bothel   96
Bourne, J. C.   66
Bowles, T. G.   180
Bowyer, R.   112, 140
Boydell, J.   85, 104, 108
Boys, T. S.   41, 66, 92, 110, 144, 156
Brayley   170
Brighton   182
Brindley, J.   96
Bristol   140
Britain   23, 26, 30, 31, 34, 36, 40, 46,
   55, 71, 98, 100, 106, 112
Britannia (Camden)   25
Britannia (Ogilby)   30
British Imperial Forces (1905)   160
British Institution   126
British Museum   75, 76
British Ornithology   102
British Seaports   83
British Wild Flowers (Loudon)   178, 179
Britton, J.   136, 140
Brooks, B.   142
Brunel, I. K.   43
Brunel, Sir I.   126
Brunswick, House of   180
Buck, S. & N.   81, 104, 110
Buckingham Palace   160

Bunbury	160	Daguere	43
Burn	22	Dalzeil Brothers	63
Burton, Captain	166	Daniell, W.	36, 130
Bury, T. T.	176	Dante	22
Byron, Lord	170	Darlington	148
		Davis, C.	90
		Davis, R. B.	146
Calthorpe, Col.	172	Day & Son	65, 172, 176
Camden, W.	25	Dayes	132
Camden Town	124	Dayes, E.	106
Camperdown, Battle of	126	de Winter, Admiral	126
Canterbury	156	Deer Stalking	170
Canterbury Cathedral	156	Delecroix	56, 59, 152, 153
Cardon	114	Denmark	142
Carington Bowles	100	Depford	150
Carlisle	134	Derby, Smith of	120
Cathedral Church of Worcester	106	Devizes	164, 182
Caukercken, C.	96, 97	Dickinson, L.	138, 156
Cawood	49, 96	Dickinson, W.	114
Caxton, W.	21, 89	*Dictionary of Artists*	89, 122
Century of Birds from the Himalaya		Diepenbeck, A.	96
Mountains (Gould)	102	Dighton's	116
Charles II	31, 96	Disraeli, B.	180
Chatelain	108	Doncaster	120
Chelsea	134	Douberg	160
Chepstow	134	Drayton, M.	25
Chesapeake (and Shannon)	146	Dresden	140
Chichester	104	Drogheda	176
China	168	Drummond, S.	126, 182
Chromo-Lithography	178	Drury Lane	170
Clarenceux, King of Arms	25	Drypoints	21, 112
Clark, J.	142	Dublin	176
Claude	104	Duncan, Lord	126
Clive, Lord	55	Durham	148
Collier Discharging	166	Dutch	28, 30
Colnaghi	114, 172	Dutton, T. G.	66, 81, 86, 166, 168, 169
Connoisseur, The	160		
Constable, J.	60, 61, 92, 104, 154	Earlom, R.	34, 58, 59
Cook, T.	98	Early English Watercolour School	106, 136
Cooke, E. W.	83, 136, 166	East Indiaman	166
Cooke, G.	136, 158, 166	Edinburgh	148, 150
Cooke, W. B.	136	Edwards, G.	102
Cooper, A.	138	Elizabethan	25
Cooper, T. S.	41, 66, 92, 156, 158	England	130, 132
Copper Plate Magazine	136	*Engravings and their Value* (Slater)	88, 152
Coronation (Queen Victoria)	162	Etching	21, 26, 28, 33, 34, 46, 52,
Cornwall	130		54, 57, 61, 104, 126, 128
Costume of Great Britain (Pyne)	128	Etching—Drypoint	54, 57
Cotman, J. S.	104	Etching—Soft-ground	37, 38, 55, 57, 108, 132
Courtnay	116	Eton	118
Cousins, S.	48, 60, 61, 114	Evans, E.	174
Covent Garden	134, 170	Eyre and Spottiswoode	182
Cox, D.	136		
Cries of London	18, 114	Faithorne, W.	33
Crimea	172	Far East	168
Crome, J.	104	Farington, J.	118
Cruikshank, G.	116	Ferneley, J.	138, 139
Cumberland, Duke of	106	*Fifty Plates of Shipping and Craft*	
Czar	112	(E. W. Cooke)	166

Finden	83, 166
Fire of London	30
First World War	81
Fittler, J.	124
Fleet Prison	23
Flint, R.	81
Forger/Fakes	83, 174
Fox	116
'Foxing'	81, 82
Fox-Talbot	43, 110
France	80, 112, 120, 132, 140, 152
French	58, 132, 152
Frome	65
Fuller, S. & J.	142
Gainsborough, T.	37, 108, 120
Gateshead Fell	144
General Post Office	148
Gentleman's Recreation	31
George III	100, 108, 116
Georgian	116
German	64
Gillray, J.	116, 160
Girtin, J.	132
Girtin, T.	36, 106, 132, 133, 134, 136
Glasgow	172
Gleanings of Natural History (1758)	102
Gordon, Gen.	138
Gosse, T.	124
Gould, J.	102
Gould, J. A.	66
Grace, Dr. W. G.	182
Grant, F.	138
'Graphic'	182
Graver	23
Graves, A.	89, 170
Graves, H.	162
Gravelot	108
Great Western Railway	162, 176
Green Valentine	31
Green (& Wigram)	168
Greenwich	76, 126
Greenwich Observatory	75
Greenwich Park	130
Greville, Hon. C.	106, 112
Groups of Cattle drawn from Nature (Cooper)	156, 157
Guest, H.	170, 171
Guildford	104, 110, 158
Hacker, E.	90
Haden, Sir S.	54
Haghe, L.	65
Hamburg	140
Hanger, G.	116
Hardcastle, E.	128
Harding, J. D.	41, 66, 92, 144, 150, 151, 158
Harral, H.	63
Harris, J.	160
Havell	36, 148, 160
Hawking	31
Hayden	81
Hayter, Sir G.	162
Heath, H. & W.	116
Heath, J.	98, 146
Heath, W.	160
Henderson, C. C.	148
Herring, J. T.	146
Hind, A.	166
History of British Birds (Bewick)	39
History of British Etching (Shaw-Sparrow)	116
History of the River Thames (J. & J. Boydell)	118
H. M. Army	146, 160
H. M. Navy	146
Hogarth, W.	52, 54, 57, 98, 122
Hole, W.	25
Holland	28
Hollar, W.	26, 28, 30, 52, 76, 91, 104
Hollway, J.	164
Holy Land (Roberts)	176
Howard, T. (Earl of Arundel)	26
Howe, Lord	77, 146
Howitt, S.	92, 93
Huggins, T.	146
Hullmandel, C.	65, 66, 102, 118, 138, 150
Humming Birds (The)	102
Humphrey, H.	116
Hunt, C. & G.	148
Hyde Park Corner	148
India	130, 162, 168
India Paper	83, 166, 154
Indian Regiments	160
Ipswich	142
Ireland	96
Ireland S.	118
Itaglio	46, 57, 65, 67
Italian	46
Itinerant (The)	106
Jansson	48
Jenkins Naval Achievements	77, 89, 112, 146
Kean	170
Kearnan, T.	170, 171
Kemble, F.	170
Kent	26, 182
King Edward	
King John	106
Kingsley, C.	138
Knight, C.	68
Knight, C. (Mezzotint Engraver)	114
Kremlin	140
Laid Down Prints	83
Laid Paper	79

Landscape	79, 89, 104	Millington, W.	41, 164, 165
Landseer, E.	68, 93	Montacute Priory	110
Lansdowne, Lord	170	Moore, J.	148
Laycock, Wilts.	43, 110	Morland, G.	58, 78, 100, 120, 122, 124
Le Blond	68		
Le Prince, J. B.	36, 57, 112, 152	Napoleonic	140, 146, 156
Lechlade	136, 137	National Gallery	98
Leighton, G.	68	National Maritime Museum	76, 91, 166, 168
Leitch, W. L.	150	*National & Sunday Schools*	164
Lewis, F. C.	132	National Trust	110
Liber Cronicorum	21	*Natural History of Uncommon Birds* (1743)	
Liber Studiorum (Turner)	58, 61, 134		102
Liber Veritatis (Earlom)	58, 61	*New Alms Houses* (1860)	164
Light Brigade	172	*New Method of Horsemanship*	96
Limestone	64	Nelson	146
Lincoln	136	Newcastle	38, 100, 144, 174
Lincolnshire	168/9	Newcastle, Duke of	96
Line Engraving	21, 22, 23, 24, 25, 26, 27,	Newmarket	138
	46, 47, 48, 49, 50, 51, 54	New Watercolour Society	144
Lithography	63, 64, 65, 66, 78, 79, 84,	Nicholl, A.	176
	90, 92, 93, 102, 118	Nicholson, F.	106
Littleton, Hon. A.	182	Nightingale, F.	172
Liverpool and Manchester Railway	78	*Night Riders of Nacton*	142
London	65, 83, 86, 91, 98	North Shields	174
London As It Is	92	Nottingham	106
London Bridge	96, 130	Nuremberg Chronicle	21
London Cries	78	Nutter, W.	114
London from Greenwich	118		
London Illustrated News	63	Ogilby, J.	30
London from Lambeth	118	*Old England*	68
London Volunteers	92	*Oriental Scenery*	130
Long, W.	90	Orme	112
Longleat	64	Owen, S.	118
Looking at Old Maps	87	Oxford	118
Loraine, F.	144		
Lords, House of	180	Paddington	162
Lorraine, C.	58	Pall Mall	170
Loudon, Mrs.	178, 179	Paris	22, 132
Lovat, Lord	52, 54, 55	Peace of Amiens	132
Lowrie	81	Pears Soap	174
Lucas, D.	59, 60, 61, 92, 154, 155	Pearson, C.	156
Ludlow	110, 154	Peel, Sir R.	42, 68
Lupton, T.	60	Pellegrini, C.	180, 182
		Pentonville	158
Maiden Lane	134	Penny, W. C. & J.	65
Malton, T.	93	Petworth	100
Map Room	75	Photographic	21, 78, 79, 82, 92, 98
Mardon's Shooting Gallery	170	Picken, T.	176
Marriage à la Mode	98	*Picturesque Antiquities of English Cities*	136
Marshall, B.	138	*Picturesque Tour of the River Thames*	118
Martial Achievements (Jenkins)	160	*Picturesque Views on the River Thames*	118
Marston Moor	96	*Picturesque Views of the Severn*	118
McLean, T.	116, 142	*Picturesque Views on the Southern Coast of*	
Medway	118, 136	*England*	136
Methuen	93	Place, F.	31, 33, 104
Mezzotint	21, 31, 32, 33, 36, 55, 58, 59,	Planographic	40, 64, 66
	60, 61, 70, 78, 80, 90, 91, 114	Plomley, R.	88
Microcosm of Great Britain (Pyne)	128, 129	Plymouth	140
Microcosm of London (Rowlandson)	122, 128	Police	68, 87, 162

200

Pollard, J. 81, 86, 148, 160
Polyolbion 25, 26
Portrait 31, 33, 79, 112, 126, 182
Portreath 130
Ports and Harbours 83
Poussin 104
Prague 26
Pretender 126
Prince of Wales 120
Print Prices Current 1926/27 138, 146
Prout, J. S. 140
Prout, S. 66, 140
Ptolemy, C. 22
Pugin 122, 128
Punch 63
Pyall, H. T. 162
Pyne, W. H. 124, 128, 176

Quakers 174
Quorn 138

Ravenet, R. F. 98
Ranjitsinhji 182
Redgrave, S. 112, 126
Reeve, R. G. 148
Regency 146, 148
Research and Reference 75
Restoration 30, 96
Reynolds, Sir J. 31, 108, 120
Reynolds, N. 23
Reynolds, S. W. 124
Richard III 170
Richardson, T. M. 144, 158
Richmond 118
Roberts, D. 93, 150, 158, 176
'Rocker' 31, 33
Rogers, J. 49
Rogers, W. 25
Romantic 152
Romney 120
Rosenberg, F. 148
Rossetti, G. 138
Rowlandson, T. 78, 92, 122, 124, 128, 160
Royal Academy 51, 52, 89, 100, 106, 108, 116,
118, 120, 126, 128, 132, 138,
144, 156, 162, 170, 176
Royal Artillery 160
Royal Astronomical Society 75
Royal Automobile Club 170
Royal Collection 106, 122
Royal College of Physicians 102
Royal Hospital 126
Royal Military Academy 106
Royal Navy 31
Rupert, Prince 31, 58, 61
Ruskin, J. 138
Russia 112, 140
Rustic Figures for the Embelishment of
Landscape (Pyne) 128

Rutland, Duchess of 31
Ryder, T. 114
Ryland, W. W. 34, 106, 116
Ryther, A. 23

St. Bride Foundation Institute 164
Salisbury 136, 154
Sandby, P. 34, 36, 106, 107, 108, 112, 132, 136,
150
Sandby, T. 106
Sartorius Family 100
Say, W. 60
Sayer, R. 100
Scotin, G. 98
Scotland 96, 130, 172
Scotland Delineated 144
Scots Fusilier Guards 160
Scots Greys 172
Scutari 172
Senefelder, A. 39, 40, 41, 66, 150, 152
Seymour, J. 100
Shannon (and Chesapeake) 146
Shaw, J. 78
Sheldon, J. 91
Shiavonetti 114
Shotley Bridge Spa 144
Siegen, L. von 31, 61, 152
Siltzer, F. 90, 91
Simkin 78, 160
Simpson, W. 172, 173
Sixty-five plates of Shipping & Craft
(E. W. Cooke) 166, 167
Size-Glue 84
Slater, H. 88, 152
Smith, G. & J. 104
Smith, J. 33
Smith, J. R. 114, 120, 121, 124, 132
Somerset, Duke of 100
Spielman, Sir J. 80
Spithead 166
Sporting Magazine 91
Stadler, J. C. 118, 119
Stanfield, C. 150, 158
Stipple Prints 21, 55, 57, 70
Stocks, L. 49, 50, 51
Stubbs, G. 100
Sudbury, Suffolk 108
Sunter, R. 139, 158
Sutherland, T. 79, 146
Swains 63
Symons, C. 146

Tate Gallery 166
Thales 22
Thames, River 118
Thames Scenery (Owen/Cooke) 118, 166
The Art Journal 68
The Birds of Asia (Gould) 102
The Hawking Party (Landseer) 68

The Humming Birds (Gould) 102
The Park and The Forest (Harding) 150
The Principal Buildings of London (1852) 176
The Queen's Visit to Jersey (1847) 176
The Railway Station 162
The Story of British Sporting Prints (Siltzer) 90

Tilt, C. 166
Tinted Lithographs 66
Toby, Uncle 49, 50
Tonal Engraving 60
Tower, The 23, 130, 158
Trowbridge 164, 165
Trustler, Rev. 98
Tuck, R. & Son 78
Turner, C. 134
Turner, J. M. W. 36, 58, 60, 89, 104, 106, 132, 134, 135, 136, 150, 154, 162
Tyburn 34

Un Forgeron 59, 152, 153
United States 178

Vanity Fair 180
Various Subjects of Landscape (Constable) 154
Varley, J. 136
Vauxhall Gardens 170
Vendramini 114
Venice 174
Victoria & Albert Museum 76, 91, 166
Victoria Queen 89, 138, 162
Victorian Britain 168
Vincent Brooks, Day & Son 180
Virginia Water 106
Vivares 124
Volumatic Marker 87

Wagstaff, C. E. 89, 162
Wales 23, 25, 79, 96, 106
Ward, I. 164, 182
Ward, J. 34
Ward, L. 182

Ward, W. 31, 114, 124
Warwickshire Avon 118
Water Colour Society 174
Water Marks 79, 80, 146
Waterloo 146, 162
Watson, C. 114
Watson, J. 148
Wellington, Duke of 170
Westall, W. 118
Westminster Abbey 130
Whatman, J. 77, 130
Wheatley, F. 78, 114
Whistler, J. McN. 92
Whitcombe, T. 146, 147
White, R. 24, 25
Whitman, A. 81, 152, 166
Wight, Isle of 130
William III 98
Williams-Wynn, Sir W. 106
Wilson, R. 104, 118
Wiltshire 41, 136, 164
Windsor 106, 118
Wood, J. 108, 109
Woodcuts 21, 22, 64
Wood Engraving 21, 61, 62, 63, 64
Woollett, W. 104
Woolwich 106
Wooton, J. 100
Worcester 63, 91, 106, 107
Worde, Wynke de- 21
Working Men's College 138
Works of Hogarth (Heath) 98
World War 158
Wove Paper 80
Wye River 118

Yarmouth 166
York 31, 81, 148, 158
York, Duke of 170
Yorkshire 96

Zinc-Plates 158

202

Notes

Notes